AUSTRALIA

LAND OF COLOUR

AUSTRALIA
LAND OF COLOUR

Text by Neil Hermes

AUSTRALIAN
PICTURE LIBRARY
SERIES

C&A CHILD &
ASSOCIATES
AN ALL-AUSTRALIAN PUBLISHER

Published by
Child & Associates Publishing Pty Ltd
9 Clearview Place, Brookvale, NSW, Australia 2100
A wholly owned Australian publishing company
This book has been edited, designed
and typeset in Australia by the Publisher

First edition 1987
Text by Neil Hermes
Captions by Dalys Newman
Photographs from the Australian Picture Library
© Australian Picture Library 1987
Printed in Hong Kong by South Sea International
Typesetting processed by Deblaere Typesetting Pty Ltd

**National Library of Australia
Cataloguing-in-Publication**

Australia, land of colour.

   ISBN 0 86777 092 9.

   1. Australia - Description and travel - 1976-
   Views. I. Hermes, Neil. II. Australian Picture
   Library.

994.06'3'0222

CONTENTS

INTRODUCTION

Perhaps 40 000 years ago or more, Australia was a vast unpeopled continent. Kangaroos grazed unmolested by dingo or man and their young were probably hunted by the Tasmanian tiger which was then found across the continent. Native cats prowled for bush birds and reptiles. Floods and droughts upset the annual rhythms and huge bushfires swept the land. The Australian environment was, however, in a 'natural balance', a concept that is now as elusive to define as finding a live Tasmanian tiger.

The continent was, and is, an ancient place. Once boasting high mountains, the landscape is now, through time and the slow process of erosion, a vast flat plateau. The hardest 'bones' of those old mountains are now exposed as rocky desert mountain ranges and the range of low mountains which divide the waters of the eastern seaboard. The Australian continent is vast, 50 per cent larger than Europe, and yet is the lowest and flattest of all the continents. With the exception of Antarctica it is also the driest.

The Great South Land was explored and settled for the first time about 40 000 years ago. We have little direct evidence of this influx, but we are able to piece together the story from fragments of evidence. The story of the first great migration to Australia has been repeated many times since by wave upon wave of new peoples and new technologies.

The first 'new Australians' were the Australian Aborigines. Their invasion of the country took perhaps 20 000 years to complete. Their origins were in south-eastern Asia and theirs was probably the first seafaring migration in the world. Slowly they settled the northern flood plains and then gradually moved down the eastern and western coasts. The most inhospitable desert and mountainous areas of the centre and south-east were the last to be inhabited. The Aborigines had a simple technology and lived as hunter-gatherers. About 6000 years ago a change swept through the Aboriginal societies and new toolmaking and technology arrived. More sophisticated hand tools evolved and Aboriginal culture developed a depth only now being appreciated by many 'European' Australians. At this time about 300 000 Aborigines lived in Australia, divided into about 500 groups or tribes. The tribes were further divided into smaller self-sufficient bands. Local groups congregated from time to time when food or water supplies were abundant or for ceremonial purposes.

The first taste of the winds of change came to the Aborigines of the coastal northern flood plains. Traders from Indonesia set up temporary camps in Australia from about 1650 onward and they had an input to the native languages and technologies. At about the same time great seafaring nations, the Dutch, English and Portuguese, were taking their first tentative steps of exploration in the region, which would eventually lead to the new wave of human immigration that continues today.

As all Australian schoolchildren learn, Captain James Cook was the first European to map the eastern coast of Australia. His reports, unlike those of the discoverers of the arid north-western coasts, were   favourable and the British interest of the time so great that within twenty years the first of the next wave of 'new' Australians were on the high seas headed for *Terra Australis*.

The First Fleet left England in May 1787 with 750 convicts of sixteen different nationalities. Most were English or Irish and these two groups have, over the last two centuries, provided the largest numbers of new immigrants to the Australian continent. Even today, over a million Australians, or 7 per cent of the total population, were born in the British Isles. Within twenty years of the first tentative settlements at Port Jackson, colonisation spread from the Illawarra Plateau to the Hawkesbury River and west to the barrier imposed by the Blue Mountains. Other settlements had been established at Norfolk Island and Hobart. Within another twenty years the whole continent was claimed as a dependency of the United Kingdom. However, the population was still small with the convict population reaching about 40 000. The shipment of convicts to Australia continued until 1867 with a total of 160 000 men and women prisoners being sent out from Britain. This had a great impact on the early character of the population but this was slowly changing as convicts received pardons and remained in the new colonies, free-settlers headed out from Europe and Australia-born families became established. By 1825 the numbers of free-settlers outnumbered convicts and the new Australian society, despite its inauspicious beginning, was starting to develop its own broader and unique character.

Gold speeded the growth of the population from a trickle to a torrent and brought great influxes of people to the continent. In 1851 the first gold was discovered and within a decade 700 000 new free-settlers had arrived. The population of Australia by the end of the great gold decade exceeded one million. In addition to British and Irish gold-seekers, many other nationalities joined the rush, the largest group being the Chinese. In 1861 over 20 000 Chinese labourers were working the goldfields of New South Wales. Most worked for wages for wealthy Chinese businessmen. Great prejudice was displayed by the Australians of European descent and many unfortunate incidents of violence against the Chinese workers darken the history books. By the end of the 1800s the only remaining large groups of Chinese goldminers were on the fields in northern Australia. Here, where the isolation and the humid and hot conditions did not welcome others, the Chinese were left to do their work. Even today a large proportion of residents of Darwin are of Chinese descent.

The first Italian to arrive in Australia was a convict, Guiseppe Tusa, who was transported on the First Fleet. Australians of Italian descent are now the third largest ethnic group in the nation. Italian-Australians first made an impact on the developing nation in the latter part of the 1800s. Some were classical musicians, others were shopkeepers and still others established themselves on the land. Many parts of the Queensland canefields and major inland irrigation areas are now peopled by Australians who trace their ancestry to Italy.

German immigrants first settled in Australia in significant numbers in the Barossa Valley from 1842 onward. Their vineyards were soon producing wines and even to this day many German traditions are maintained in the valley. Although South Australia was the first destination for many German immigrants, some families moved to the southern districts of New South Wales and established wheat and sheep properties.

Pakistanis came to Australia in the latter part of the nineteenth century, bringing camels with them. For eighty years the Afghans, as the Pakistanis were known, and their camels, were responsible for transport of goods throughout the inland. The Afghans were a colourful and characteristic symbol of the arid outback during its exploration and first settlement, but unfortunately very few families remained and very little of their culture entered the general Australian society until the influx of migrants from the Middle East in the last forty years. Their contribution to Australia's development is best remembered in the name of the train, the Ghan, which now transports freight and people to the continent's Red Centre.

The Kanakas were Pacific Islanders who came to Australia as the flow of convict workers came to an end. They first came to New South Wales on ships fitted out by a pastoralist, Ben Boyd, and although they were supposed to come freely, some of the operations looked very much like the slave-trading of the previous century.

Quite a few Kanakas found their way to the Riverina and in the 1860s a Sydney merchant, Captain Towns, imported Kanakas to work on his experimental rice plantation near Brisbane. Eventually the greatest numbers of Kanakas were concentrated in the sugar-growing areas of coastal Queensland and their contribution to the development was considerable. It is estimated that upwards of 50 000 came into Australia in the second half of the nineteenth century.

With the White Australia policy formally entrenched in the early years of the Commonwealth, laws were passed to prevent the inflow of Kanakas and an active policy of repatriation was followed.

The turn of the century and the creation of the Federation of Australian States brought more changes. Different groups of new immigrants began to arrive in significant numbers. Lebanese and Greeks were establishing communities and European Jews were looking for new homes, away from persecution in Russia and Poland. Many fled to the United States but some also headed to Australia.

Prior to 1901 there was no distinctive Australian ethos. A scattering of individual colonies and isolated groupings of peoples of other homelands lived and worked on the island continent. Most looked to countries thousands of kilometres away for their identity. Federation changed that. At first the change was slow but from the crucible of the Great War an Australian identity emerged. Now, 87 years after federation and two centuries after the first European settlement, it is probably fair to say that most Australians see themselves as Australians first. Some are Queenslanders, Territorians, Sydneysiders, Greek-Australians or Aborigines, but all are Australians.

The Australian population is still changing. Post-World War II immigration has created about 40 per cent of the current population. The character of the immigration over the last few decades is now also changing. Whereas soon after World War II most immigration was of Europeans, mainly Greeks, Yugoslavs, Poles, Hungarians and Czechs, by the late 1970s a greater proportion of Asians were entering Australia. Many were refugees from Indo-China, but they included Indians, Malaysians, Chinese and Japanese. Many 'old' Australians have objected to this change, claiming that Asian immigration will be a divisive force in the ever-evolving Australian society. Whatever the rights and wrongs of that argument, Australia is now seeing itself as much more a part of Asia than an outpost of European motherlands.

Australia is a country of great diversity—Australians both new and old, a vast ancient landscape, and unique plants and animals. It is hard to select one place or thing which encapsulates the range of characteristics that represents the spirit of Australia. One measure is to look at international recognition given to uniquely Australian places and things. Six areas in Australia have been recognised by UNESCO as having 'outstanding universal cultural and/or natural heritage values'. Four of these—the Great Barrier Reef, South-West Tasmania Wilderness, Lord Howe Island and East Coast rainforests of northern Queensland—are included in the list on the basis of their natural heritage values. One, the Willandra Lakes district of New South Wales, the site of the discovery of the oldest human remains in the world, is listed for its cultural values. Only one place, Kakadu National Park, is internationally acclaimed for its universal cultural and natural attributes. In addition, Kakadu is owned by a group of the first Australians, the Gagadju Aboriginal peoples, and is now also the home of many 'new' Australians. It is a place of great beauty, of great artistic antiquity, and in many ways it brings together much of what is truly Australian.

Kakadu is a magical place. Spread from Van Diemen Gulf east of Darwin to the cliffs of Arnhem Land, the park is over 7000 square kilometres of wetlands, sandstone cliffs and plateaus, rainforests and woodlands. About a thousand types of plants and a third of Australia's bird species are found within the park. The vast wetlands are inhabited by over fifty fish species including barramundi and archerfish. The waters are also home to one of the most dangerous animals in the world, estaurine crocodiles. Palm-like pandanus trees line the watercourses and a profusion of flowering plants like grevilleas, hibiscus and turkey bushes abound. Unlike most other Australian trees, many of Kakadu's species lose their leaves during the long Dry Season.

One reason for the World Heritage status of Kakadu is the rich diversity of Aboriginal art sites. There are over 5000 art sites scattered through the park, and they are now internationally recognised as being the oldest and largest collection of early human artistic creativity. Excavations of Aboriginal occupation sites have discovered edge-ground stone axes over 20 000 years old. But, in addition to this great prehistoric richness of human society, Kakadu is still the home of modern-day Aborigines. They own the land, live in it and maintain much of their traditional lifestyle.

Uranium has been discovered within the Kakadu region and in 1980 the Ranger mine was opened. A new town was built and Australians are being drawn from all parts of the country to extract the ore.

Many lessons of the past have been heeded. The needs of the Aboriginal people have been respected and met and uranium ore is being extracted with proper safeguards to protect the unique ecosystems of the region. Tourist development is, to date, proceeding in an orderly and non-destructive way and the third largest town in the Northern Territory, Jabiru, is growing and developing its own character.

Kakadu is in many ways a microcosm of what Australia was and is. Hopefully, the future of Kakadu and the future of Australia will be a balance of the interest of Australians of different backgrounds and a balance of development with protection of the landscapes and wildlife that make the continent such a special place to all who make it their home.

THE BIRDS

To the casual observer, Australia's brilliantly coloured parrots, the flightless emu and perhaps the giant of the kingfishers, the kookaburra, characterise our unique birds. However, when we look beyond the showy colours, the large size and the raucous laughter of these familiar species, Australia's birdlife has even more of interest to offer.

Many groups of birds are found in Australia and nowhere else in the world. This is so of the lyrebirds, plains wanderer, treecreepers, magpies, currawongs, magpie-lark, bowerbirds and emu. Other groups, although found elsewhere, are well represented in the island continent and these include penguins, albatrosses, tropicbirds, parrots and cockatoos. Not only are the types of birds of great interest but their behaviour patterns set them apart from birds elsewhere in the world. Who could not be amazed by the mallee fowl which lays its eggs in a huge compost heap and then carefully tends the mound to ensure that the correct temperature is maintained, or by the bowerbird which constructs an elaborately decorated display arena to lure a mate.

These unique qualities of Australia's birdlife can be attributed in part to the long isolation of the continent from the rest of the world. In addition, Australia's changing climate over millions of years has created new opportunities that birds have exploited. For example, as the inland became drier some species adapted to a desert way of life and others became restricted to the wetter coastal zones.

Of Australia's 700 or so bird species, over half are found nowhere else in the world. Some are exceedingly rare and are the subject of rescue programmes, for example, the noisy scrub-bird in Western Australia and the Lord Howe Island woodhen. Other native species have benefited from European settlement of the landscape and become problems to pastoralists or orchardists, for example, the silvereye. Unfortunately, over twenty species of birds from other parts of the world have been introduced by man into Australia and many of these are serious pests both to agriculture and to native birds, for example, the common starling, common mynah and feral pigeon.

Australia's largest bird

The emu is a distinctive Australian and Australia's largest bird. It shares a position on the Australian Coat of Arms with the red kangaroo. Although flightless, emus are not handicapped by this. Not only can they walk long distances to find food (distances of many hundreds of kilometres), they can also run at speeds of up to 50 kilometres per hour. Pairs form in the summer months and the female lays up to twenty eggs during the winter. She then abandons the male who does all the caring for the eggs and chicks. During the eight weeks of continuous incubation he may lose up to 8 kilograms in weight. After the eggs hatch he then cares for the distinctly striped young for up to a year and a half. In Western Australia large numbers of emus move from the drier pastoral zone into wheat country, causing considerable damage. Many forms of control have been attempted by the farmers. However, the most dramatic, and the least successful, were the infamous 'Emu Wars' of 1932. An army squad with two Lewis guns set up a series of emu drives which killed less than 200 birds at a cost of 10 000 rounds.

Cassowaries, large flightless relatives of the emu, are found only in thick rainforests of northern Queensland and New Guinea. The Australian cassowary is a handsome bird. The feathers are black, head and neck are blue and a pair of red wattles hang from the throat. The head is topped with a large casque. An adult can stand up to 2 metres tall. Cassowaries are generally solitary birds preferring the safety of the thick forests. Occasionally, when the natural rainforest fruits are in short supply, they will enter gardens and eat cultivated fruits.

Cassowaries are known to be aggressive and can kill people. They are strong kickers and the foot is armed with a lethal spike. Although aggressive behaviour is usual only during the breeding season some individuals appear to be generally belligerent.

We now turn from the flightless cassowary of the tropical jungles to the southern ocean and the largest flying bird alive today—the wandering albatross. With a wingspan

9

of some 3.5 metres and its effortless flight the wandering albatross must be the 'ultimate' flying machine. Albatrosses are typically birds of the southern oceans, although three species do occur in the northern Pacific Ocean and individual birds have been rarely recorded in the North Atlantic. Eight species of albatross are known in Australian waters and most nest on islands in the sub-Antarctic. The wandering albatross is typical. It breeds in islands such as Macquarie Island well to the south of Tasmania. Wandering albatrosses nest every two years since it takes almost twelve months to raise one chick. If an egg is lost early in the season the adults may attempt to nest again the following year. Outside the breeding season the adults and immature birds leave the sub-Antarctic waters and feed in waters around southern Australia, South Africa and Tierra del Fuego. In the winter months it is not unusual to see concentrations of feeding albatrosses around the southern coasts of Australia. The concentrations off Sydney have been studied for many years by ornithologists. The researchers chase albatrosses in small boats and capture them with nets before they can get airborne. By placing numbered bands on the bird's leg much valuable information on the habits and wanderings of the birds has been gathered. Banding studies suggest that wandering albatrosses may live up to thirty-five years.

Similar studies have been conducted on the shearwaters or muttonbirds which nest on islands in southern Australia, particularly Bass Strait. Called muttonbirds because the young are harvested and eaten, shearwaters are dark brown seabirds with long, slender wings like albatrosses. Shearwaters nest in burrows dug into the grasslands and breed in vast colonies. The short-tailed shearwater has a remarkable life cycle. All females lay their single egg between 20 November and 1 December and many individuals lay on the same day every year. After hatching the chick is abandoned during the day and fed only at night. The chick can grow to double the size of the adult birds. The adults then abandon the chicks and they starve for a period of about two weeks before they emerge from the burrow and take to the wing and the sea. What then occurs is even more remarkable. The whole shearwater population migrates via New Zealand and the central Pacific Ocean to the waters north of Japan. Some birds reach the Bering Sea. Having spent the southern winter in the northern Pacific Ocean the adults return to the same Bass Strait island breeding burrow to lay on the same date again! Large numbers of young birds perish on their first migration which is a round trip of about 30 000 kilometres.

The harvesting of the chicks by the Bass Strait Islanders is a traditional activity which is now strictly controlled. Known numbers of birds are taken as chicks from the burrows and the effect on the total shearwater population has been calculated to be negligible. The chicks are plucked and sold either fresh, frozen or salted for human consumption. Oil from the stomachs is used to produce suntan lotion, the fat is given as a food supplement to cattle and the down is the principal source of down for Australian-made sleeping bags.

An unusual pelican

The Australian pelican is a popular and friendly bird. It often develops a particular understanding of our pastimes and learns where to wait for handouts of fish. The Australian pelican has behaviour patterns which make it unlike the pelicans that occur on most other continents. Its breeding is adapted to the irregular pattern of rainfall which characterises much of the dry Australian continent. Breeding may occur at any time of the year and may be delayed for years until suitable conditions are present. Large colonies nest on islands in Lake Eyre and other inland lakes after wet years. Unfortunately, breeding is often too successful and as the inland dries up, large numbers of young pelicans find it difficult to obtain food. At these times pelicans can become quite bold and appear on ponds in city parks or even on swimming pools in their desperate efforts to find food.

Flocks of pelicans often feed together in a highly organised manner. They swim slowly together and drive shoals of small fish into shallow water and then simultaneously dip their bills to catch their food.

Close relatives of the pelican are the tropicbirds. Three species live in the tropical oceans and islands of the world and two, the red-tailed and the white-tailed tropicbirds, occur in Australian waters. Tropicbirds are very tame during nesting and will allow close approach. This, added to coloured bills and black and white plumage, makes them distinctive and well-known seabirds. In flight their tail streamers, which may be up to half a metre in length, add to their appeal.

Storks are another group of birds with great appeal even if they are given legendary capacity beyond the biologically possible! Typically, storks are large, long-legged black and white birds with brilliant red colourings. This is all true of Australia's only stork, the jabiru. Found in marshland from the Kimberleys through the tropics and down the eastern coast to around Sydney, the jabiru is usually solitary or seen in pairs. This is unlike storks overseas which often form sociable flocks. The jabiru is a versatile feeder and lives on a range of aquatic animals such as fish, frogs, crayfish and lizards. Typical of storks everywhere, jabirus build large and bulky nests placed high in a tree.

The dancing brolga

Similar in stature to the jabiru, Australia's most common crane, the brolga, is a much more finely built and statuesque bird. In addition the brolga has an elegant and inspiring courtship dance. Songs and poems have been written in recognition of these inspiring displays. One Aboriginal legend claims that the brolga was once a famous dancer but having declined the advances of an evil spirit was changed to a stately brolga. The brolga's dances appear to be passionate affairs. The pairs face one another and bow and bob as they move towards and away from one another. Occasionally one bird will trumpet wildly with its head held back. The most spectacular routine is when they leap into the air kicking their legs forward and then gracefully glide back to earth. Remarkably, these performances do not occur during the breeding season but they are presumed to form a part of continued reinforcement of the pair bond.

Brolgas share the inland waterways with about twenty species of ducks, geese and swans. These waterfowl display an amazing range of adaptations to the varying reliability of rainfall across the continent. Along the eastern and southern coasts where winter rains are reliable and in the tropical north where the summer Wet Season is the norm, waterfowl have regular breeding cycles. However, through most of the continent, the inland ducks are erratic breeders and have adapted to respond quickly to flooding whenever it occurs.

The magpie goose is characteristic of the waterfowl of the tropical north. A distinctive large black and white goose it feeds on vegetation in swamps and billabongs. When the Wet Season comes, large tracts of low-lying country are flooded, producing vast fields of swamp plants suitable for young geese. Breeding occurs in huge concentrations and the nest is a floating platform of vegetation. The colonies form as protection from dingoes which take many young geese. As the Dry Season approaches, the adults and young head back to the permanent waterways. This yearly cycle is typical of other northern waterfowl such as the tree-ducks, Burdekin duck and diminutive pygmy geese.

In the coastal areas of southern Australia, where winter rainfall is reliable, there is a regular pattern of winter and spring breeding of some waterfowl species, for example, the maned duck, Australian shelduck and chestnut teal. These species usually nest in hollow trees near permanent water.

A curious group of ducks, the diving ducks, are also regular breeders. The musk duck and blue-billed duck live on permanent deep waterways. They feed on small aquatic animals which they catch while diving. They can remain submerged for up to 60 seconds. Since they live on large permanent waterways breeding can occur on a regular annual basis.

The remaining Australian ducks, including the grey teal, black duck and rare freckled duck, breed only in response to favourable weather conditions. Concentrations of these birds occur on the large inland lakes and rivers and, as rains fall and flooding begins, so breeding commences. It can be at any time of the year. These species are also quite adaptable in their nest requirements. The grey teal will nest on the ground, in trees, under rocks and even in rabbit burrows! If flooding occurs the lack of a suitable nest site will not deter the grey teal from breeding.

Australia's main game-shooting birds are the black duck and the grey teal. Since they are both species which have irregular breeding strict annual bag limits are set based on annual duck counts by wildlife authorities.

A strange swan

Perhaps one of Australia's most distinctive waterfowl and one which attracted the most interest from the first white settlers is the black swan. Since Northern Hemisphere swans are white, this black antipodean emphasised the stark differences of their adopted new land. The unfortunate black swan was under some criticism by the homesick Europeans. George Bass, the noted explorer, wrote:

> That song, so celebrated by the poets of former times excellently resembled the creaking of an ale-house sign on a windy night.

Birds of prey, the hawks, falcons and eagles, have never been celebrated by the poets on their musical calls. In fact the calls of most raptors are at best whistles but usually harsh screams. Australia's largest bird of prey is the wedge-tailed eagle. This close relative of the North American golden eagle has a wingspan of up to 2.5 metres. Like its American cousin, the wedge-tailed eagle had a reputation for being a major predator of domestic livestock. Research has shown that although live lambs are occasionally taken they are usually sickly and dying anyway. Most lambs taken by eagles are usually already dead from other causes. Very occasionally a young eagle will take a healthy lamb but the impact on sheep production is quite insignificant. Wedge-tailed eagles prefer to feed on wallabies, rabbits or lizards. Carrion is an important component of the diet.

Australia boasts another large eagle, the white-breasted sea-eagle which floats over most coastal areas, patrolling for fish, sea-snakes, waterbirds and other small animals. This eagle shares the coastal skies with another fish eater, the osprey. This bird is very rare in other parts of the world and the subject of elaborate protection measures. Although not common in Australia, the osprey has not yet become an endangered species. The thick coastal rainforests are home to white goshawks and crested hawks. Further inland we find many species of kites and falcons.

Black kites are great scavengers and wherever you find a rubbish tip, abattoir or stockyard you will have a quota of these inquisitive birds. Inland bushfires often attract large flocks of black kites which prey on the scattering wildlife. The kites are often a hazard to fire spotters working from aircraft around the fire front.

The falcons are tenacious birds. The Australian hobby falcon, although only 30 centimetres in height, will attack much larger birds such as ducks and galahs. At the nest the fiery-spirited bird will attack any intruder. The author can vouch for its determination. To inspect a nest 15 metres up in a tree required protective clothing including a leather jacket, gloves, goggles and crash helmet!

The fascinating mallee fowl

A much safer bird to study is the remarkable mallee fowl. This large ground-dwelling inhabitant of the dry inland mallee scrub has fascinated scientists for decades. The mallee fowl's scientific name is Greek and literally means 'I abandon and desert my eggs'. On the surface it may appear that the mallee fowl is a vagabond but nothing could be further from the truth. The mallee fowl's life is constant toil. The female bird spends virtually all her time searching for food in order to produce her large eggs. This is exhausting work, for she may lay up to thirty-three eggs in the course of the summer breeding season and the country is dry and parched. The male has an even more demanding task, that is, to maintain the nest mound. The mound is a heap of rotting leaves, twigs and soil about 4 metres in diameter and up to 1.5 metres high. The eggs are laid into the centre of the mound. The male dutifully checks the temperature of the nest on a daily basis. In the spring when fermentation in the nest is high the mound is opened up to allow heat to escape. In summer, earth is heaped onto the mound to insulate the eggs. These excavations are all done by scratching and many cubic metres of material are moved back and forth each day. The tiny chicks never see their parents. After hatching, the chick digs unaided to the surface of the mound and immediately has to care for itself. It can fly within 24 hours! Life certainly wasn't meant to be easy for a mallee fowl!

One of the least known and rarest Australian birds is the plains wanderer. Although rather unspectacular in appearance, it looks a little like a quail and is of great scientific interest. The plains wanderer has no close relatives anywhere in the world and is classified in a group of its own. Its known home country is the grasslands of inland southern Australia, which are now heavily stocked with sheep, cattle and rabbits. The plains wanderer is probably vulnerable to attack by cats, dogs and foxes. This bird is now the subject of much research activity by the Royal Australian Ornithologists Union.

Another once rare bird, but one which has now been rescued, lives on the delightfully beautiful Lord Howe Island. The Lord Howe Island woodhen is a reddy-brown ground-dweller the size of a bantam. It is flightless since it had no natural predators on its island paradise. That is, until man arrived. The first settlers ate the birds and many sorry tales were recorded. In 1788 Thomas Gilbert wrote:

> Partridges [woodhen] ran in great plenty...several of these I knocked down, and their legs being broken, I placed them near to me as I sat under a tree. The pain they suffered caused them to make a doleful cry, which brought 5 or 6 dozen of the same kind to them, and by that means I was able to take nearly the whole of them.

Introduced cats and pigs soon removed most of the remaining birds from the island.

In 1979 only thirty woodhens remained and these were on the peak of the highest mountain. In 1980 nine birds were flown by helicopter from the mountain peak to a specially constructed compound on the island's lowland. Within three years ninety-two chicks were produced. As the chicks matured they were released to parts of the island from which pigs had been removed. Woodhens are now well established in many areas on the island where they hadn't been recorded in living memory. This great achievement is one of the few real success stories in attempting to rescue a very rare bird species through captive breeding.

'Help save the poor Bustard.' So reads the slogan on a promotional shirt produced by wildlife authorities trying to protect the little-known bustard. He is a large bird standing over a metre tall and with a wingspan of up to 2.5 metres. Bustards of one species or another occur throughout Africa, Europe, Asia and Australia. Being large ground-dwelling species that favour grasslands they are now threatened by many agricultural practices. In some parts of the world they are hunted for sport. Although bustards can fly well, they prefer to rely on camouflage for protection. When first disturbed by a predator or human, the large bird 'freezes' in the long grass. If the intruder makes a closer approach the bustard will cautiously stalk away still hoping to avoid detection. Only if really pressed does the bird finally start into a run and launch itself into flight. In Australia bustards are nomadic and most likely to be seen in the arid tropical north.

A small world

The twentieth century is supposed to be the century of travel. With the coming of large aircraft and relatively cheap fares, the world is now a smaller place. Australia is part of this world trend and is becoming a more popular destination for tourists. But Australia has been on the Asian tourist route for centuries. Every year, hundreds of thousands of international bird visitors fly into Australia from Asia and the Pacific. They are the migratory wading birds and range from the tiny red-necked stint weighing less than 25 grams to the eastern curlew measuring more than half a metre in length.

The migratory waders number over thirty different species and travel straight-line distances of up to 15 000 kilometres twice each year. A typical migratory wader is the sharp-tailed sandpiper. Weighing in at less than 100 grams it is perhaps more distinctly coloured than is typical of this notoriously plain group of birds. Its feet are yellow and its head rufous with the rest of its body boldly marked brown and black. Tens of thousands of these little birds feed on mudflats around the southern capitals during the Australian summer. As autumn approaches they feed furiously, adding about 30 per cent in weight in preparation for the long journey ahead. The sandpipers then form into large flocks and head north, probably via the Kimberleys or the Top End. From there we know little of their route through south-eastern Asia except that by May all the birds are on the breeding grounds in Siberia! Amateur ornithologists have captured and banded thousands of sandpipers. One bird caught near Sydney during February was found dead in April on the southern coast of mainland China! Amateur research efforts in Perth have resulted in returns from Siberia!

Other species of migratory waders travel annually between Japan and Australia. Since the long-term survival of these international bird species depends on human activities in countries in different hemispheres, international co-operation is required to protect them and their living places. The governments of Australia, Japan and China have agreements which commit themselves to these goals.

Terns are probably best known from the large colonies nesting on cays within the Great Barrier Reef. Some such as the sooty tern nest on the ground and others such as the white-capped noddy make seaweed nests in low trees. This bird is well known on some of the reef's resort islands. Terns feed on small fish which they catch by diving from a height above the water.

Australian parrots are among the most beautiful birds in the world. However, since many are very common, their beauty is often highly underrated. If the crimsom rosella, the rainbow lorikeet or even the galah was a rare bird its beauty would be highly praised. Such is the penalty of familiarity.

Australia has been called *Terra Psittacorum*—the Land of Parrots. Everyone has their favourite parrot, be it the bizarre palm cockatoo of the rainforests of Cape York or the confiding rosellas of a city garden.

The not-so-familiar budgie

Internationally the best known Australian parrot is the budgerigar. To one Aboriginal tribe it was the 'betcherrygah' to use one highly Anglicised spelling. To one of Australia's earliest and greatest ornithologists this small green parrot was known as the 'Warbling Grass Parakeet'. We can only wonder as to whether the budgie would ever have become a popular cagebird struggling under that name! Anyone used to only a single blue or white budgie living in a cage would be amazed to see the bird in its natural surroundings. Green buderigars are all that are known in the wild, no yellows or blues or whites. And where a single talkative bird is all that one would normally expect as a household pet, in the wild, flocks are numbered in the thousands. For the household bird a flight across the kitchen might be a marathon, but for its wild relatives hundreds of kilometres may be covered in the desert searching for seeding grasses and water. The contrasts of lifestyles could hardly be greater.

Sulphur-crested cockatoos are also popular cagebirds and this is due in part to their ability to mimic human speech. Having fed well, birds living well away from cities and towns often 'entertain' themselves by aimlessly tearing leaves and bark from trees. Unfortunately, this activity has been further developed by city-living cockatoos. They now 'entertain' themselves by tearing insulators from TV aerials, stripping putty from window seals or tearing up furniture or verandahs built of western red cedar. As can be understood, this has made sulphur-crested cockatoos extraordinarily unpopular birds with some people. They are viewed as being so destructive that they have been described as 'birds with bolt-cutters attached to their heads'. It is probably good practice in cities to observe sulphur-crested cockatoos from a distance and not encourage them to feed in suburban gardens. So long as the birds are busy looking for food less casual damage is likely to be caused.

Another popular parrot, which is often encouraged to feed at bird tables with no damaging results, is the rainbow lorikeet. Found along the eastern coast from Cape York to Adelaide this lorikeet has attained particular international stardom. At a reserve owned by the Queensland National Trust on Queensland's Gold Coast, thousands of rainbow lorikeets are fed every day. At eight in the morning and four in the afternoon the sky is filled with wheeling flocks of these brilliant blue, orange and green birds. They come in from the forests up to 30 kilometres away for their handouts of bread, honey and water. The birds are so keen to feed that it doesn't concern them who holds their food dishes. Every year thousands of people get pleasure, not only from seeing and photographing these brilliantly coloured birds at close range, but from having the birds perch all over them while they are feeding.

To small birds of the bush the melancholy call of the pallid cuckoo is a frightening sound. The calls continue during the season all day and all night. The cuckoo will not attack them but like cuckoos around the world it robs them of the chance to rear their own chicks. Over eighty different species of bush birds, including honeyeaters, whistlers and robins, play unwilling host to the cuckoo's offspring. The young cuckoo is so demanding that its adoptive parents will continue to push food into its gaping mouth despite its growing larger than themselves. Birds other than the foster parents are sometimes even allowed to give the bird a feed.

Australia's largest cuckoo is a very strange bird. The pheasant coucal was known to the early settlers as the swamp pheasant. It is a heavily built, long-tailed cuckoo which seems to crash from tree to tree rather than fly. Not only does the power of flight elude this cuckoo but it also rears its own young! Coucals are found in wet coastal country from Sydney north to beyond Darwin.

The cold nights are full of strange sounds besides cuckoos. Some of the owls have eerie calls described by their bush names; for example, the barn owl is also called the screech owl, and the barking owl is known to some bushmen as 'screaming woman'! Around the major cities the most frequently heard owl is the boobook or 'morepoke,' which has a repetitive two-part call like its name.

A distinctive large-eyed wide-mouthed night bird often mistaken for an owl is the tawny frogmouth. Although they can look alarming with their mouths open wide this bird is the master of camouflage. During the day a bird sitting motionless on a branch can look like a dead, broken tree branch.

The bushman's clock

Two species of kookaburra inhabit the Australian bush. The familiar laughing kookaburra or 'bushman's clock' is found along the coast from Cairns to Adelaide and Tasmania and Perth. The blue-winged kookaburra inhabits the tropical north, and as well as its bright blue wings it is distinguished by not laughing. The kookaburras are the largest kingfishers in the world. Most kingfishers, true to their name, live near water and eat fish. But not the kookaburras. They have adapted completely to a bush life and they live on insects, lizards and sometimes small snakes.

Kookaburras often become quite tame and line up in suburban gardens for handouts of meat or cheese. Once a regular beat is established parent kookaburras often bring their offspring along for a handout as well.

Another truly Australian bird which is well known for its song is the superb lyrebird. Although normally shy, in some places, notably Sherbrook Forest near Melbourne, the birds will allow visitors a close viewing. The male builds a display mound which is just a small clearing in the forest. When the winter breeding season approaches, the males use the display mounds to perform elaborate dances and song routines. The long tail is arched over the bird's head and produces a spray of feathers in the shape of a lyre.

The courting males prance about and vibrate the delicate tail feathers in a brilliant, shimmering display. A loud, rich song accompanies the dance. In addition to the male's own repertoire, he mimics any favourite sounds which he feels may impress his mate. It may include the songs of other birds or man-made sounds such as woodchopping or engine sounds. One remarkable bird learned to mimic a flute. Since the birds mimic one another the flute sound has now been incorporated into the repertoire of a group of neighbouring lyrebirds.

The focus of all this is to attract the female to the male's territory. Mating takes place on or near the mound and the female is then on her own to build the nest, incubate the eggs and raise the young.

Of all the brilliantly coloured small bush birds the ones which appeal to most people are the delicate fairy wrens. Around the capital cities of the south-east, the superb fairy wren makes his home. The breeding male is a cocky little bright blue and black. Like the female he has a long, narrow tail which is held at right angles to the body when perching. The females and immature males are a dull grey in colour and the female has a touch of red about the face. Since the superb fairy wren lives in family groups and only the mature male is brightly coloured it was often assumed that the one male had many females. This is not the case but it did not stop these wrens being called 'Mormon wrens'.

Wrens have a complex family structure which means they can produce many young when conditions are favourable. The one family group can produce many young in a year since the breeding male and the immature males and females all take part in caring for the young. Superb fairy wrens are friendly birds to have about a suburban garden but they are vulnerable to attacks from domestic cats.

Many of this continent's bushland birds share names with birds from the Northern Hemisphere. It must have made the early settlers feel less abandoned to give well-known bird names to the unfamiliar birds.

Hence Australia has robins, warblers, flycatchers, choughs and magpies which are quite unrelated to their northern namesakes. For some other new birds the apparent similarities were with several inhabitants of the Old World and we now have groups of Australian birds known as quail-thrushes and cuckoo-shrikes.

The Australian magpie family is a good example of how new names evolve. It contains a number of familiar and distinctive black and white birds—some are called magpies, after a superficial resemblance to magpies of the Northern Hemisphere; some are named currawongs, after their calls; and the butcherbirds are named for their eating habits.

The Australian magpie is both loved and hated. It is a large and inquisitive bird in the gardens and parks of many cities. They can become quite tame and enter houses for food. Unfortunately, magpies can become quite aggressive during the breeding season. Some birds defend the territory vigorously. The main method of defence is to swoop low over any intruder and let out loud calls of bill clacking. This can be quite off-putting and very annoying if the magpie's territory includes your backyard. Many curious techniques are observed to ward off swooping magpies. In Canberra, where this problem is acute, it is not uncommon to observe public servants walking to work holding an umbrella over their heads on a fine spring morning. Children similarly may be observed wearing hats, especially hats with 'eyes' drawn around the brim. The theory is that if magpies attack only from the rear, which seems usually to be the case, the novel headgear will deter the avian aggressor. Such are the birds (and people) of Australia.

The sulphur-crested cockatoo (Cacatua galerita). *Flocks of thousands of these white cockatoos with fine sulphur-yellow crests are commonly seen out on the plains and in open forest country.*

The colourful king parrot (Alisterus scapularis) *grows to 45 centimetres and is fairly common in coastal forests and near rivers. This bird nests in large trees and timber milling is endangering its habitat.*

A ground-feeding bird, the long-billed corella (Cacatua tenuirostris) *is found in open timber country and is becoming increasingly rare.*▼

The young male red-tailed cockatoo takes four years to acquire his magnificent adult plumage. Common in forests and open timber country, the bird advertises its presence with an extremely rowdy call.

Probably the most plentiful parrot in Australia, the budgerigar (Melopsittacus undulatus) *forms into enormous flocks, flying in tight precise formation. They are a common sight on the open plains.*

Frolicsome and friendly rainbow lorikeets.

Rainbow lorikeets (Trichoglossus haematodus) *feed in the tops of flowering native trees and are conspicuous for their noisy screeching and incessant chatter.*

The eclectus parrot (Eclectus roratus) *is found mainly in forests and jungles in the northern regions of Australia.*

Cockatiels (Nymphicus hollandicus) *are also known as cockatoo parrots and quarrions. They are frequently seen by the roadside, often on telephone wires, and have an attractive whistling call.* ►

The Major Mitchell cockatoo (Cacatua leadbeateri). *These birds are rare, found only in isolated spots in dry inland areas.* ▲

Often seen at groves of tall banksias, the slow-flying yellow-tailed cockatoo tears pieces from rotting tree limbs to extract wood borers and grubs.▼

The largest of all the parrots, the palm cockatoo (Probosciger aterrimus) *has a powerful beak with which it cracks open nuts from palm trees. When disturbed the bird 'blushes', its cheek patches turning a deeper red.*

A flock of galahs takes to the sky. The entire flock will 'change colour' as they wheel, revealing the beautiful pink under-feathers. Today, the galah is one of the most prolific of inland birds.

The emu is among the few birds of which the female is liberated. She does the courting,
the male looks after the young. The female lays a clutch of about nine eggs and the male sits
on them for about eight weeks until the chicks emerge. He is then also responsible for their
upbringing.

Emus (Dromaius novaehollandiae) are Australia's largest bird and the world's second
largest after the ostrich. Almost always found in flocks, stalking majestically across inland
plains or open forest country, emus are non-flyers but can run as fast as a galloping horse.
(Previous page.)

The butcherbird (Cracticus nigrogularis) is *so-called because of his habit of 'hanging up' his meat. Often he will tightly wedge his dead prey, or other items of food, into tree forks.*

Bird of a thousand voices, the lyrebird (Menura novaehollandiae) *is the prince of mockingbirds—it mimics all bush noises. The bird's outstanding feature is the tail of the mature male which is made up of sixteen striking feathers. The male rakes up a dancing mound about a metre wide from soft soil and struts around it to impress the female, a small homely bird lacking any adornment. (Following page.)*

The brush turkey (Alectura lathami) *is one of Australia's unique mound-building birds. These remarkable constructions are made to hold the eggs and provide enough heat for hatching.*

King of Australia's kingfishers, the kookaburra (Dacelo gigas) *is also called the Laughing Jackass. Its laughter resounds at sunset and sunrise throughout the bush, in towns and many suburban areas.* ▲

Although belonging to the kingfisher family, the kookaburra rarely catches fish, preferring to dine on insects, snakes, rodents, lizards, yabbies and the young of other birds. ►

The richly coloured sacred kingfisher (Halcyon sancta) *is commonly found in mangrove and open timber country, near creeks and rivers. It announces its arrival with a ringing four-syllable call, a repeated 'ki'.*

The noble wedge-tailed eagle (Aquila audax), *Australia's largest bird of prey.*

Increasingly found in urban areas, the white-plumed honeyeater (Lichenostomus penicillata) *is a noisy, pugnacious fellow whose distinctive 'chick-o-wee' is a common garden call.*

The bold, inquisitive Lewin honeyeater (Meliphaga lewinii). All honeyeaters possess a brush-like tongue for sucking honey from blossoms.

The nankeen night-heron patrols shallow swamps, lake shores and river edges during the night, hunting for fish, frogs and crustaceans which it catches with its long pointed bill.

The white ibis (Threskiornis moluccanus) *is often seen flying in formation. Also called the sacred ibis, this bird is very similar to that recognised as the sacred bird of the ancient Egyptians.* ▲

The brolga, Australia's only native crane, has had a great influence on Aboriginal life and culture. The bird's dancing has inspired the choreography of several corroborees, and the dancers' dress and make-up imitate the big colourful bird. ▼

Gannets—big birds of the sea. Talented divers, gannets will plunge into the sea from great heights of 20 metres or more. ◄

Often seen soaring high above the coastline and inland rivers, the white-breasted sea-eagle (Haliaeetus leucogaster) *is a strong flyer with a wingspan of about 2.3 metres.*

A greedy bird, the black cormorant (Phalacrocorax carbo) *will sometimes eat until it is too heavy to take off.* ▼

The shy and elusive jabiru (Xenorhynchus asiaticus) *is the only member of the stork family found in Australia.*

Sooty terns on Michaelmas Cay, Queensland. Often called sea-swallows, terns are smaller than gulls, with more finely shaped wings and beaks, and a typical swallow-like flight.

The beautiful sight of pelicans floating on calm waters has provided inspiration for many artists and poets. Pelicans are found throughout Australia. They feed in a close circle, constantly moving to stir the fish and prevent their escape at the same time. (J. Baker & APL.)

The black swan (Cygnus atratus) is found throughout Australia except in the extreme north. The bird's colour is accentuated by a red bill and white highlights on the wings.

Seagulls—the scavengers of the air—are seen mainly on the seashores with occasional appearances inland. ▼

Until the Dutch explorer Willem de Vlamingh discovered the black swan in Western Australia in 1697, the black-coloured swans were unknown. Today, in parks and gardens throughout the world, the Australian black swan is as well known as the white swan of Europe.

Looking like something left over from Halloween, the masked owl (Tyto novaehollandiae) is found in savannah country and is popular in some areas as a rabbit destroyer. ➤

The mallard duck (Anas platyrhynchos) has been introduced into Australia in small numbers and is found in parks and garden pools.

The tawny frogmouth (Podargus strigoides) *is an odd-looking bird with a wide gaping beak and soft plumage.*

The tawny frogmouth is one of nature's great camouflage artists. The birds can sit or crouch along the branch of a tree, blending perfectly into the overall picture.

Australia's most common owl, the boobook (Ninox novaeseelandiae) *is a woodland bird whose pleasant 'book-book' call can be heard almost anywhere in the bush at night. (Following page.)*

THE ANIMALS

In 1770 Captain James Cook tried to put into writing his amazement at the strange creatures he had encountered in the new continent that he was exploring:

> Besides the Animals, which I have before mentioned, called by the natives Kangaroo, or Kanguru, here are wolves [dingoes], Possums, an Animal like a ratt, and snakes, both of the Venemous and other sorts. Tame animals here are none except Dogs, and of these we never saw but one, who frequently came about our tents to pick up bones, etc. The Kangaroo are in the greatest number, for we seldom went into the country without seeing some.

And this was only just the beginning. It was about thirty years later that the platypus was discovered and this caused a scientific storm that lasted a century. At first, many of Australia's animals were believed to be hoaxes and this was especially so of the platypus. Once these strange creatures were accepted as real, the scientific battles began as to their relationship with other animals. There were carnivorous animals like cats that had pouches, huge bats that looked like foxes, poisonous snakes and fish that breathed air through lungs.

Of course many of the first reports of Australian wildlife appeared in the diaries of the Dutch explorers of the continent's northern and western coasts. The first written description of a kangaroo is attributed to William Dampier who, in 1699, landed at Shark Bay in Western Australia. He wrote:

> The Land-Animals that we saw here were only a sort of Racoons, different from those of the West Indies, chiefly as to their legs; for these have very short fore-legs; but go jumping upon them as the others do (and, like them, are very good meat).

This description is of one of the smallest of the kangaroo family, the banded hare-wallaby which is now restricted to two islands in Shark Bay.

The paradoxical platypus

The platypus probably caused most controversy when it appeared on the nineteenth-century scientific stage. The first animals were discovered in the Hawkesbury River, north of the infant Sydney colony in 1797. One of the discoverers wrote in his diary that he believed the creature to be a type of amphibious mole. One of the first scientists to examine a skin of a platypus called it 'paradoxus' based on the furry coat, duckbill and webbed feet. How justified he would have felt if he had known that this new little aquatic Australian also laid eggs and suckled its young with milk!

Once scientists accepted that the platypus did in fact exist, the debate as to where it fitted into the animal kingdom raged for decades. The platypus laid eggs but was warm blooded and so could not be a reptile. Since it had no feathers it was hardly a bird. But how could a furry warm-blooded mammal lay eggs? The issue was finally resolved when it was discovered that the platypus also produced milk for its young, even though the milk oozed from the female's body rather than coming from teats. The platypus was a mammal, albeit a very strange one.

The leathery bill of the platypus not only locates food but is highly sensitive to touch. In the murky waters where platypuses live, hearing and sight are senses which are of little value. In fact, platypuses close their ears and eyes when submerged. All information about location and feeding is sent to the animal's brain via the highly sensitive bill. Most of the diet consists of various insects and other aquatic invertebrates.

When not in the water, platypuses spend most of their time in short burrows located just above the water level. A separate, more complex burrow is built for nesting.

Two eggs are laid and the female incubates them by holding them against her body with her tail. The young hatch in a few weeks and then spend four or five months being fed milk from the numerous ducts on the female's body.

Although still found in most coastal districts of eastern Australia the platypus is considered to be vulnerable. There is a danger that the species is disappearing slowly as rivers are dammed and urban and industrial developments have their effects on the coastal rivers.

The other egg-laying mammal is the echidna. In fact there are two species of this extraordinary ant-eating specialist: one in Australia and the other in New Guinea. Echidnas are often incorrectly called anteaters or porcupines but this is quite misleading since they are certainly not related to either of these American or European animal groups.

Like the platypus, the echidna is a mammal; that is, it has warm blood, has hair and suckles its young on milk. Unlike the platypus, the echidna doesn't lay its egg in a nest. The egg is deposited in a pouch, similar to those of marsupials. How the echidna does this is still not known. When the female lays the egg the body is probably doubled up and the egg laid directly into the pouch. The claws appear to be useless to help in this task. The egg then hatches in the pouch and the young is carried for as long as the poor mother can bear the spikes! The young is then left in a suitable hiding place until old enough to feed on its own.

The sluggish echidna has developed a fine protective coat made up of long pointed spines. These cover the whole upper surface of the body, although the underbelly is still only soft skin covered in hair. To protect this vulnerable area the echidna has developed two highly effective behavioural characteristics. The first is to roll completely into a ball. The head is tucked in with the tail and all that is exposed to the enemy is a ball of spikes. It is extraordinarily difficult to unroll an echidna that has wrapped itself up like this. The second escape route, and the one preferred by the echidna, is to dig into the ground a little way and only leave the spiky body exposed. Once an echidna has a grip on the ground it is again almost impossible to budge it.

These defence ploys mean that echidnas have few, if any, natural enemies, although dingoes and goannas may take the occasional echidna and Aborigines often collect them.

Echidnas are highly specialised in their eating habits. They live solely on ants and termites, or white ants. The Australian bush is full of the earth nest mounds of termites and these are often seen to have excavations on the surface. This is evidence of echidna activity. The echidna breaches the base of the mound with its strong front claws. The tongue is covered in a sticky saliva and this collects the milling termites. Like the platypus, the echidna has no teeth and the termites are ground up on the bony surface of the mouth.

Surprisingly, perhaps, echidnas are still widespread throughout the continent and although it is not particularly numerous there is no concern about its ability to survive.

The world's favourite Australian

It would be hard to separate the koala from kangaroos as Australia's most prominent ambassadors. Although it is the Flying Kangaroo that adorns the tail of Qantas aircraft it is the koala that stars in much of Australia's promotional tourist advertising overseas. Koalas have also been subjects of some international diplomacy with 'ambassadorial' animals sent to Japan and the United States in recent years. Unfortunately, some of these animals have died, which adds to the koala's chequered history since the time of European settlement.

Because of their nocturnal lifestyle, koalas spend the day asleep in the fork of a tree. This, together with their generally cuddly appearance, promotes the perception that koalas are docile and gentle animals. Nothing is further from the truth as many publicity-conscious politicians have discovered when cuddling a koala for the ever-present photographers. The sharp, strong claws are adapted for very agile climbing but can be put to other use!

Koalas are widespread on the eastern coast of Australia and are limited to places where their preferred food trees are found. Although the preference is eucalypts, and in particular river red gum, grey gum, swamp gum and blue gum, other types of trees are eaten at times. Koalas will drink water but they usually obtain all the water they need from their leafy diet.

There is evidence to suggest that koalas evolved from ground-dwelling animals, such as the modern wombat. How else can you explain the fact that koalas have downward-opening pouches and no tails, surely both disadvantageous to an inhabitant of the treetops. The koala is, however, remarkably well equipped for its gum leaf diet. The digestive system is unlike those of other mammals and can cope with the oils that gum leaves contain.

The story of the koala over the last two hundred years has been one of changing fortunes. When Europeans first arrived, koalas were widespread and common but kept in check by dingoes and Aborigines. As the Aborigines became more reliant on European food supplies and dingoes were shot, the koala population was suddenly able to expand unchecked. By the end of the last century, koala numbers were so high that a large fur trade was established. In 1924 the colossal number of two million koala skins were exported. In many areas uncontrolled shooting eliminated whole groups of koalas. As urban and agricultural development fragmented the forests into small pockets the remaining koalas suffered from other stresses. The preferred food trees died out under pressure from koalas, and dogs and cars took their toll. A small population of koalas survived in some northern suburbs of Sydney for many years until finally succumbing to a combination of these pressures.

Koalas now have a new threat. Although disease would have been a part of koala life in the past, for small populations of koalas under stress, disease is now of major concern. Fortunately a major credit card company has recently funded research into this problem in Australia and the Japanese are investing large amounts of money in studying the animals they have in their zoos.

Mention possums to most Australians and they immediately think of brush-tailed possums and the nuisance they can be when they use our houses as theirs. But the possums are a group of over twenty different animals.

The smallest possum is the little pygmy possum weighing less than 10 grams and small enough to sit on the palm of your hand. Its bigger cousin, the burramys or mountain pygmy possum, is one of the rarest mammals in Australia. Its story is interesting since it was first reported from fossils found in a cave. For over seventy years it was believed that this animal no longer existed until one turned up in a ski hut at Mount Hotham in Victoria. A small population is now also known to live near the summit of Mount Kosciusko. Burramys live beneath the snow in the winter, making tunnels in the buried vegetation. As the skiers are working hard at staying on their skis, burramys are busy staying alive in the snow beneath them. The survival of burramys within the ski fields depends on careful planning, especially concerning machine-packed ski runs and summertime activities.

The brush-tailed or common possum has a rather easier lot in life. Where it can it gets into the roofs of houses and plays havoc with the sleep of other residents. You see, possums are nocturnal and this is a large part of the problem. However, resolving to remove possums from your roof may be only the start of the problems. One unscrupulous entrepreneur offered to trap and remove possums from houses for a fee. The trapping worked well but the possum-catcher then released the villains into a nearby suburb where they took up new residences. The possum-catcher's services were then required again and the possums were returned near to their 'original homes'. The original complainants were assured that these were new possums moving into the vacated area and the cycle began again. Perhaps everyone was content. People were having possums removed from their homes, albeit for a short period, the possums were well travelled and well fed and no doubt the possum-catcher was happy!

Kangaroos are another group of Australian animals where the number of different species is often underestimated. More than fifty kinds are known and they are all restricted to Australia and New Guinea.

The large red and grey kangaroos are well known to all Australians and around the world. A kangaroo appears on the nation's Coat of Arms and a Flying Kangaroo adorns the tail of all Qantas jets. Some kangaroos are extinct, some rare and some so common as to be pests. Most live on the ground but some live on cliffs and others in trees.

The smallest of the kangaroo family, the musky rat-kangaroo, is a miniature kangaroo and not related in the slightest to rats. It is an inhabitant of the rainforest floor around Cairns and weighs about 500 grams.

The hare-wallabies are kangaroos about the size of hares. Two species are extinct, two are very rare and the spectacled hare-wallaby is still found in the open country of northern Australia.

In appearance, much more like kangaroos 'should look' are the rock-wallabies. However, unlike the 'proper' kangaroos, rock-wallabies are more like goats in their habits.

Most suitable parts of the country, with the exception of Tasmania, have or had a local species of rock-wallaby. Many are distinctively marked and all are highly agile on steep rock faces. The yellow-footed rock-wallaby is brightly coloured and marked with yellow limbs and tail and prominent black and white patches. Its home is the arid rocky ranges of central South Australia, far western New South Wales and central Queensland. The more widespread black-footed rock-wallaby is a popular tourist attraction at Simpsons Gap National Park near Alice Springs.

A little-known group of kangaroos are the tree-kangaroos. Although centred on New Guinea two species occur in far northern Queensland. They live in rainforests and are well adapted to their tree-dwelling existence. Nobody could claim they were agile climbers; however, in their own way they are efficient at getting about in the trees. They also spend a considerable amount of time feeding on the ground.

The larger and typical kangaroos are variously known as wallabies, wallaroos and kangaroos. There are no strict differences except that the wallabies tend to be smaller and the kangaroos the larger species. The wallaroos fall somewhere in between.

Typical of the wallabies is the red-necked wallaby. Standing about 50 centimetres high and with a tail some 65 centimetres in length this is the common wallaby of the forests of south-eastern Australia. The neck has a rufous wash. The tips of the muzzle, toes, tail and paws are black. Otherwise this wallaby is generally grey.

The gestation period of the red-necked wallaby is about thirty days. The young will remain in the pouch for up to ten months. The female may become pregnant again while there is a youngster in the pouch but the gestation will be interrupted. The unborn young will not be born until the young living in the pouch leaves permanently. The unborn youngster may remain in a suspended state for almost a year. This adaptation is common among the kangaroos. It enables them to respond quickly to favourable weather conditions and is insurance against the loss of pouched young.

The big red and the blue flier

The largest of all the kangaroos is the red kangaroo. The male is usually brick-red in colour and the female, sometimes called the 'blue flier', is blue-grey. Large males can be quite massive. The total length from nose to tip of tail is up to 2.5 metres. Large males can weigh up to 85 kilograms.

Red kangaroos are found throughout arid Australia. Feeding is usually at night and although they do drink at stock troughs and dams, they can exist without water when on green food. Red kangaroos are able to modify their breeding patterns to suit the climatic conditions. During drought, breeding stops altogether and when conditions are flush, breeding is maximised. A female red kangaroo can have an out-of-pouch young still suckling on one teat, a pouched young living on another and an embryo in a suspended gestation in the uterus. Among the remarkable adaptations that enable this breeding pattern is the female's ability to produce different compositions of milk suitable for ages of the two young.

The red kangaroo and several other kangaroo species are the subject of a controversial culling and commercial-use programme. Large numbers of kangaroos can have a major impact on commercial agricultural production. A detailed system of assessing kangaroo numbers has been developed, and permits are given for property owners to remove fixed numbers of problem animals. Under strict regulation some of these animals are then allowed to be used commercially.

It is an emotionally charged issue. The animal welfare groups are strongly against the culling, arguing that the kangaroos are threatened, that the killing of the animals is cruel and that wildlife should not be exploited.

However, if the issues are examined carefully it will be seen that not only can a sustainable, humane kangaroo industry be maintained but that it is in the interests of nature conservation that it be allowed to continue.

In any discussion of kangaroo harvesting, it is important from the outset to define 'kangaroo'. As has been already discussed, the kangaroo family includes a large number of species, some common, some rare and some already extinct. 'Kangaroo' here refers to the three large commercially harvested species: the red kangaroo and the eastern grey and western grey kangaroos.

Large numbers of these species exist and are mainly concentrated in sheep country. Surveys early this decade indicated a total nation-wide kangaroo population at about 20 million animals. Drought can reduce these numbers by around 40 per cent. But this is the norm for kangaroos whose remarkable breeding biology is designed to take advantage of good seasons when they come. Even an annual harvest of several hundred thousands of animals fails to stop an increase in animals in good seasons. We now have good scientific data to demonstrate that annual harvesting of the three large kangaroo species is sustainable indefinitely. The historical facts support this. In the last fifty years over one million skins have been exported on average annually. There is no sign of decline in the kangaroo population.

Arguments of cruelty are not supported since within moments of being spotlighted, commercially harvested kangaroos are shot. This compares with the days of yarding, trucking and culling of sheep and cattle that are taken to an abattoir. Finally it seems irrational to try to draw a moral line between utilisation of kangaroos, or other wild animals, and domestic stock. Isn't the difference purely conceptual and how does that justify one and not the other?

A major deleterious effect of the campaigns against kangaroo harvesting is that it takes effort away from the important conservation issues. Many of the smaller kangaroos are endangered and need urgent attention. While we fight conceptual battles real animals are disappearing.

Despite the great diversity of the native animals the early settlers for various reasons felt a strong urge to introduce familiar animals from their old homelands. Sometimes, as is the case of releasing pigs and goats on remote islands, it was to ensure the survival of anyone becoming shipwrecked in the future. Sometimes, as with foxes and rabbits, it was to provide sport. In other situations animals were introduced as beasts of burden, hence the populations of wild camels and water buffaloes. Finally, many exotic animals such as black rats were accidentally introduced to their new homes.

Who could have believed that the humble European rabbit would be so successful and so destructive in its new home? First released in 1858 for sport shooting, the rabbit spread within sixty years to cover half the continent. Even with modern control techniques including poisons and myxomatosis the impact of rabbits on agricultural production and native animals is still high. Pigs, goats, cats and donkeys also have their economic and ecological impacts.

The stories of water buffaloes and camels in Australia have an ironic twist. Both species were introduced to Australia and both cause significant damage (very severe in the case of the buffalo). Australia has large wild populations of both these species and now exports animals back to their original homes. In the case of the camels the only wild animals anywhere in the world are in central Australia and small numbers are exported to Saudi Arabia.

The most widespread exotic animal and the one that may cause the greatest environmental damage is the feral cat. Descendant of domestic felines they are now truly wild animals. They are most active at night and feed on live animals up to the size of a brush-tailed possum. Unfortunately the feral cat is now well established from the rainforests to the desert.

Not all snakes are venomous. Despite man's instinctive fear of snakes there are many species of snakes that are quite harmless. These include the file snakes, blind snakes, tree snakes and others. The largest snakes in the country, the pythons, are also not venomous but very large specimens could be dangerous since they kill by constriction. Australia's largest snake is the Oenpelli python which can grow to over 6 metres.

However, it is the dangerous snakes that capture the attention of most people.

Venomous snakes

Until recently it was believed that the taipan of coastal Queensland and the Northern Territory was Australia's most deadly snake. It is found in a range of habitat types and feeds at night as well as during the day. Prior to 1955, when an antivenom became available, bites were invariably fatal and many deaths occurred. The taipan has been recorded at over 3 metres long and is very fast across the ground.

A snake which was first tested in 1975 has been found to be four times deadlier than the taipan. It is the small-scaled snake which fortunately is found only in arid sparsely settled country in central Australia. This snake is a thousand times more toxic than the diamondback rattlesnake of North America.

Another highly dangerous and distinctively shaped snake is the death adder. This species is found throughout mainland Australia and has an immediately recognisable 'viper' shape. This snake prefers to conceal itself in leaf litter or soil and leave its tail exposed beside its waiting mouth. As small animals wander by, it twitches its tail to lure them close for attack. Fortunately this snake, like most, rarely attacks humans unless deliberately provoked.

Sea-snakes are common in tropical waters and are highly dangerous. Most attacks occur when the snakes are being handled on a beach or when the snake is accidentally caught in fishing nets.

Australia's largest lizards are known locally as goannas. In Africa and Asia they are known as monitor lizards and include the world's largest lizard, the komodo dragon. The Australian bush is full of tall stories concerning long goannas. Goannas are supposed to relish the idea of escaping from danger by running up the bare legs of female pursuers! Also, if a goanna bites you, be warned that the wound will reopen on the seventh anniversary of the bite! As with many bush yarns, there is an element of truth in the stories.

When frightened. goannas run up the treetrunks or fence posts as a means of escape. Also, since goannas eat carrion, a bite will often become infected and keep reopening. None of Australia's goannas are dangerous unless they are forced to bite or scratch when cornered.

A large group of Australian lizards are known as dragons. Two members of the dragon group are quite unmistakeable. The thorny devil is a tiny desert-dweller which is covered in spiny scales. It is a slow-moving little lizard that hunts ants during daylight hours. It is an animal strongly associated with inland sand-dunes and could be a symbol for Alice Springs and the Red Centre. Preferring the wet tropics, the frilled lizard is a dragon which can reach a length of over 2 metres. This big lizard is usually encountered on the ground where it searches for insects and other small animals. When alarmed it faces the intruder and raises its frill which almost totally surrounds its head. This gives the lizard the appearance of great size and can deter a would-be predator. If a hurried retreat is required, the frilled lizard raises itself onto its back legs and makes for the nearest tree.

Skinks, geckos and legless lizards make up the rest of the lizard families.

The dangerous crocodile

The recent worldwide successes of the Australian film *Crocodile Dundee* starring Paul Hogan has thrown a previously little-known ancient Australian into the spotlight—the estuarine crocodile. Unfortunately this publicity has been fuelled by a number of recent fatal crocodile attacks. Few people realise that the estuarine crocodile is the most dangerous crocodile in the world and also one of the most dangerous animals in the world.

The estuarine crocodile is found throughout south-east Asia, Indonesia, New Guinea and the south-west Pacific. The most viable population, however, occurs in northern Australia, centred on the Northern Territory. The smaller Johnston's crocodile is found in the same areas but feeds entirely on fish.

Estuarine crocodiles give no warning of attack. The prey, usually wallabies or other small animals, is usually taken from the water's edge. The crocodile locates its prey and then approaches from under the water. In a surge of power the reptile launches up to several metres from the water and clasps the victim in its vicelike jaws. The crocodile then heads back to deep water where the victim is drowned. If the prey is large the reptile may back into the water while rolling—the infamous death roll. This has the effect of stunning the victim and reducing its chances of escape.

When in crocodile country precautions should be taken to avoid attack. It would certainly be foolish to swim in waters known to contain estuarine (also unwisely known as saltwater) crocodiles. Estuarine crocodiles live much of their lives in fresh water many kilometres from the sea. It is also sensible not to be involved in any activities designed to attract wild crocodiles. Some unscrupulous tour operators feed wild crocodiles, which places not only their paying customers at risk, but also other river users. It is also good practice not to leave food scraps such as cleaned fish around boat ramps. This only encourages crocodiles to frequent places where fishermen and other boat users gather.

After years of uncontrolled hunting crocodiles were fully protected in Australia in about 1970. The numbers are now building up again. Careful plans are in place to keep cities, towns and properties clear of dangerous animals while at the same time guaranteeing the long-term survival of these remarkable relatives of the dinosaurs.

The inland rivers stock some of the most interesting and popular sports fish anywhere in the world. However, the total numbers of freshwater fish species are not large, owing to the dry nature of the continent.

The Queensland lungfish is a sluggish metre-long inhabitant of the coastal rivers of central Queensland. Unlike most fish, this predator breathes air from the surface of the water. The lungfish has gills as well as lungs.

Several species of eels frequent the coastal rivers as well. Typical of freshwater eels, breeding occurs in the ocean and very long migrations are undertaken for the young to return to the ancestral freshwater rivers.

Perhaps the most famous freshwater fish of inland waters of southern Australia is the giant Murray cod. Specimens have been recorded at 113 kilograms and today fish of about 30 kilograms are still regularly caught.

Breeding by Murray cod is triggered by rising floodwater in spring. Up to 40 000 eggs are laid among the debris on the bottom of the river. The adult fish feed mainly on other fish and shellfish.

The number of these Murray cod has declined over the years and this has been attributed to overfishing and the effects of introduced fish. The greatest likely factor is the controlling of the river flow by artificial dams.

Unfortunately, despite the good fishing to be had with our home-grown Australian fish, the lure of the Old Country has been too great for the fishing fraternity. English perch, rainbow trout and brown trout have been released into many Australian streams. Despite our experience with the devastating effects of the release of other foreign animals into the Australian environment government agencies still sponsor the release of exotic fish. Often the same government agencies are responsible for the control of other exotic species. It seems a strange paradox.

Among the invertebrate animals, the Australian continent is just as uniquely endowed as with the more advanced feathered and furred species.

Over fifty different species of termites, or white ants, are to be found here. A termite's mound is the home of a large number of infertile worker termites and a single pair of breeding adults. The social order is similar to that of a beehive with a single fertile queen.

Termites live on wood and underground tunnels are dug linking the mound with the food source. Where the mound is in a tree the tunnels are within the wood of the tree. Termite mounds are remarkable pieces of engineering. The outside layer of the mound is solid earth which insulates against high temperatures. In very hot climates, galleries are built in the outer layers of earth and filled with good insulating material such as stored food, waste products or lengths of grass. In addition the mounds are built in such a way that the hottest sun does not hit the mound directly. Convection currents are set up which draw cooling air through the mound; a termite-designed air-conditioning system! The central living galleries of the mound are thereby maintained at a constant temperature.

Deadly spiders

In addition to many unique spiders, Australia has the dubious honour of being home to the most dangerous spider in the world.

It is the Sydney funnel-web and male spiders have caused deaths in children in less than two hours. Fortunately the spider is large and relatively easy to distinguish. An antivenom became available for bites of this funnel-web spider in 1980. In the past it was usually children, elderly people or pregnant women that were most at risk from the bites of this spider.

Red-back spiders are found throughout Australia and are also highly dangerous. Deaths have occurred from bites of this spider; however, no fatalities have been recorded since antivenom became available in 1956. The female spider is highly distinctive, possessing a bright red spot on the black body. The Australian red-back spider is a close relative of the dangerous black widow spider of North America and the katipo of New Zealand.

Gum leaves are the koala's main food and vast quantities need to be eaten to supply the animal with its quota of nutrients. To cope with such dietary demands, the koala has an appendix about 2.5 metres long.

The koala usually gives birth to a single young which is carried on the mother's back after five to six months in the pouch. (Lone Pine Sanctuary, Brisbane.) (Previous page.)

The Aborigines named this cuddly-looking creature 'koala' meaning 'I don't drink' because the gum leaves it eats supply all the moisture it needs. (Lone Pine Sanctuary, Brisbane.)

The koala's tail is replaced by a callused pad which enables it to sit for hours in the fork of a tree without discomfort.

Baby kangaroos—joeys—live in their mother's pouch until able to hop at her feet. Even then, when threatened with danger the joey will tumble quickly into the pouch for protection.

Boxing kangaroos. A very game fighter, the kangaroo uses his powerful buttress of a tail for support and kicks forward, striking with the nails of his two great toes.

Tree-kangaroos, members of the genus Dendrolagus. *These unusual marsupials found in north-eastern Queensland and New Guinea are well adapted to life above the ground.*

Red kangaroos—most widely known of Australia's marsupials. These kangaroos graze in mobs on the open plains and when in danger move at great speed, hopping on their hind feet with bounds as long as 8 metres.

As the dry season sets in across northern Australia wildlife becomes concentrated at the drying pools. ▲

Wallabies are usually found in hill or scrub country and apart from being smaller than the kangaroo they share the same characteristics. ▼

The charming little pademelons are mainly nocturnal, camping under logs and in thick vegetation during the day. (Bottom right.)

The yellow-footed rock-wallaby (Petrogale xanthopus)—an extremely acrobatic animal whose main home is the rocky ranges of northern and central South Australia. ►

Ring-tailed possums (Pseudocheirus peregrinus) *have long prehensile tails, often carried rolled into a tight ring shape when not being used for climbing.*

The lumbering wombat is an active burrower, sheltering in holes during the day and emerging at night to feed on grass, herbage and roots. ▼

The sugar glider (Petaurus breviceps) *is probably the most abundant of Australia's 'flying' marsupials.They are tough, adaptable creatures with a widespread habitat.*

Ring-tailed possum. Australia has many varieties of pouched animals which live in trees and feed on honey, flowers or foliage. Although some species look similar to the American opossum they are not closely related and the correct name for the Australian variety is phalanger.

Once fairly common across much of mainland Australia, the western barred bandicoot (Perameles bougainville) is now reduced to a very few small colonies such as Bernier and Dorre Islands in Shark Bay, Western Australia.

The Top End rock rat (Zyzomys argurus).

Termite mounds in the Northern Territory. Northern Australian termites are the most primitive and largest in the world, being about 3 centimetres long. Their enormous homes are masterpieces of fantasy and sculpture, with structures often towering over 6 metres. They are built of earth particles joined together with saliva, and when dry they have the hardness of concrete.

The platypus (Ornithorhynchus anatinus) *is a unique combination of reptile, bird and mammal.They inhabit freshwater rivers and lagoons from Tasmania to northern Queensland.*

One of the real wonders of the animal world, the echidna has a long tongue coated with sticky fluid which it inserts into ant holes. When withdrawn, the tongue is covered with hundreds of ants.

The dingo does not bark like the ordinary dog but makes a sustained, dismal howl and that only at night. His ears are always erect, his tail is bushy and his canine teeth are usually longer than those of the domestic dog. Their colour varies but is normally a tawny yellow with paler belly, white tail tip and feet.

Dingoes are believed to have inhabited Australia for more than 10 000 years and have so far eluded man's attempt to conquer them. The wild dog, although eradicated from many of the southern pastoral districts, still has a wide territory in northern and central Australia.

Fruit bats form 'camps' consisting of thousands of individuals who fly great distances in search for food, always returning to their home base.

Unique to Australia, the Tasmanian devil (Sarcophilus harrisii) is an ancient marsupial predator. About a metre long, this stocky creature is less ferocious than it looks. It is found in the isolated highlands of Tasmania.

Camels running wild near the Olgas. Introduced from India in the nineteenth century, camels proved invaluable in the development of the arid interior of Australia for more than half a century. Displaced by motor transport, the few that remain mostly roam free.

Water buffaloes roaming free in the Northern Territory.

These sharp-toothed, small-eyed saurians have become a rather gruesome tourist attraction in the north of the continent. There are two species of crocodiles: the relatively harmless freshwater crocodile and the more lethal saltwater variety.

The tree-frogs of the Australian bush are noted for their night concerts when the air comes alive with a rich chorus of sound.

A banksia provides a resting place for a small native frog.▼

The taipan (Oxyuranus scutellatus) *is one of the most lethal in the world. Found in northern Queensland, it can grow to more than 3 metres and has fangs almost a centimetre long. The taipan carries an enormous quantity of venom—enough to kill 200 sheep.* ▲

A sandhill python basks in the sweltering heat near Ayers Rock. There are nine species of python in Australia. (Following page.)

Introduced into Queensland in the 1930s to combat the spread of the sugarcane beetles, the cane toad is now well established along Queensland's coastal regions and in north-eastern New South Wales.▼

The common red-bellied black snake is venomous but no fatalities have been recorded in adults. ◄

Confident of its ability to ward off attacks, the harmless thorny devil lizard (Moloch horridus) *basks openly in sand patches.*

The large lace lizard, or goanna, can grow as long as 2 metres. (Following page.)

The king brown snake, one of about 160 distinct species of snakes that are found in Australia. ◄

The sand goanna (Perentie-varanus giganteus) *is found in northern and central Australia and can grow as long as 2.4 metres.*

The most spectacular of Australia's reptiles, the frilled lizard (Chlamydosaurus kingii) *uses its amazing Elizabethan collar to bluff attackers and as a storehouse for food. The insects it catches are kept in the folds of the collar until required.* ◄

The strange-looking bearded dragon lizard is a stoutly built fellow up to 60 centimetres in length. He relies upon camouflage for protection, rarely running from danger. ►

Very large and fast moving, the non-poisonous huntsman spider is often found inside homes and is commonly called a 'tarantula'.

One of the most poisonous of Australia's spiders, the red-back has a body the size of a large pea and is a relative of the black widow spider of North America.

The aggressive funnel-web spider is the most deadly spider in Australia. They spin a silken T-shaped funnel in their burrows and when cornered rear up with fangs opened ready to strike.

THE RUGGED INTERIOR

The inland will never be the same. Ayers Rock, for decades a symbol of the solid, tough, pioneering spirit of Australians, had, for many, been seen as a white Australian symbol. First 'discovered' by Europeans in the 1870s it was named Ayers Rock by William Gosse in 1873. And yet, for thousands of years the rock already had a name. To the local Pitjantjatjara and Yankunytjatjara Aboriginal people it was Uluru and was an integral part of their 'religious traditions'. These traditions link these peoples and Uluru with Aboriginal peoples from a vast area of inland Australia.

In 1985 the inalienable freehold title to Uluru National Park (including Ayers Rock) was given to the traditional Aboriginal owners of the land. This marked a recognition by the Australian white community of the great significance the land has in Aboriginal society. Arguably the most recognisable international symbol of the Australian inland, the Rock is back in the hands of the first Australians. Our history has turned a page.

The original Aboriginal settlement of Australia occurred about 50 000 years ago, probably from the Indonesian archipelago. It seems likely that the founding population were castaways who drifted ashore in the north or north-west of the continent.

Archaeological finds at Lake Mungo

At Lake Mungo, in south-western New South Wales, the world's oldest remains of truly modern man (*Homo sapiens sapiens*) were discovered in 1969. Subsequent archaeological finds in the area have shown that as early as 30 000 years ago religious practices were involved in the burial of the dead.

Lake Mungo is now recognised as one of Australia's six World Heritage areas. The others are the Great Barrier Reef, Kakadu National Park, Lord Howe Island, the East Coast rainforests of northern Queensland, and south-western Tasmania. Lake Mungo's significance is due to its importance in our knowledge of human evolution. Members of our species were hunting along these once food-rich lake shores about 26 000 years ago. At that time a young woman died, she was cremated on the beach and her bones broken and interred in a round hole. Her remains were discovered by archaeologists and are evidence of the oldest known cremation ritual anywhere in the world.

This area is now arid desert with no sign of the lakes, swamps and billabongs which were once common. The desert winds are exposing the ancient human camp sites, fireplaces and burial pits. These winds have also produced wonderful eroded landscapes, reworking the old lake beach sands and creating new landscapes, for example, the ridges dubbed the Walls of China.

The cremation practices at Lake Mungo are the earliest evidence yet of what developed into religious traditions that people refer to as the Aboriginal Dreamtime.

Dreamtime, or Dreaming, is the beginning of the world and is the basis of Aboriginal religion and social life. According to Aboriginal lore, the world was created by the totemic ancestors of today's Aborigines. These part human, part animal beings travelled across the landscape building mountain ranges and digging our rivers and billabongs. The land was entrusted to the people by these creators—Aboriginal people don't own land; the land owned them. It could not be sold but was handed down from generation to generation, along with the creation stories.

Dreaming beings were the main themes in Aboriginal art. Rock art and engravings are found throughout Australia, wherever suitable surfaces exist. The Wandjina style of the Kimberleys and the X-ray and Mimi styles of western Arnhem Land have become world-famous examples of primitive art. Art in Australia predates the ancient art sites of Europe by thousands of years and are the world's most ancient examples of abstract expression. Bark paintings are still being produced by artists in some Aboriginal communities where the traditional lifestyle remains relatively intact.

The Aborigines were a nomadic people, following the seasons around their country, gathering food and holding ceremonies to appease and please the ancestors. The sacred and the profane were inextricably intertwined in the everyday business of life.

Despite the technology of Aboriginal society being one of the simplest in the anthropological world it was both effective and appropriate to their lifestyle. It allowed them the mobility needed in order to maintain their economic and ritual activities throughout the year's hunting cycle.

Most well known among Aboriginal weapons are the boomerangs. Used for hunting, as a musical clapping instrument and, in the case of the returning boomerang, as a form of entertainment, boomerangs have a variety of designs. Hunting boomerangs are often not symmetrical and are thrown directly at larger prey such as emus, kangaroos and wallabies. Hunting boomerangs are not usually of the returning type.

At the time of European settlement there were about 500 000 people in Australia speaking about 500 languages. Many languages have now died out, especially in the east and south of the continent where European settlement has been longest and most intensive. Although massacres were a part of the decimation of the Aboriginal people, the diseases inadvertently brought in by the settlers were the major killers. Influenza, smallpox and venereal diseases spread rapidly through Aboriginal settlements and since they had little resistance to these new strains, the tolls were heavy.

After a long period when the policy towards Aboriginal people was based on ideas of assimilation, self-determination is now the predominant approach towards Aboriginal affairs. An integral part of this policy has been the granting of land rights to Aboriginal communities. Recognising the great religious significance of land to specific groups of Aboriginal people, most State governments have started returning some traditional lands to their original 'owners'. The return of Uluru to the people of the area is a step in this direction. The desert country of Uluru National Park is now again being managed like it has been for thousands of years. Traditional collecting of plant fruits and hunting of desert mammals, emus and lizards is now again part of the landscape.

The desert environment was a hard one, even for Aboriginal people. The vast Tanami Desert north-west of Alice Springs supported only one person per 100 square kilometres. In coastal country of the Northern Territory, where the sea and tidal rivers provide large and continuous amounts of food, the average could be as little as one person every 25 square kilometres. Deserts were harsh places for plants, animals, Aborigines and the first European explorers.

Of all of the continent's deserts perhaps the one that challenges Australians most is the Simpson. Sitting astride three States, the Simpson is, however, often far from being a lonely and remote spot.

The challenge of the desert

Although first crossed only by expeditions on camel, the area was crossed with vehicle tracks in the 1960s during extensive geological surveys. Although still a dangerous place for the unprepared or inexperienced, the Simpson Desert is now regularly crossed by tourists and scientists alike using four-wheel-drive vehicles.

Some modern-day adventurers use rather less conventional means to cross the desert. Ron Grant crossed the desert by foot in 1985. In temperatures of up to 58 degrees Celsius he took five days to cover the 379 kilometres. His was a successful crossing; however, many less well-prepared adventurers underestimate the power of the desert and succumb to the heat and dryness.

On the eastern edge of the desert is another famous inland landmark. Birdsville, a tiny town with a police station and one hotel, is a quiet place 364 days of the year. On the day of the annual picnic races, however, the town is visited by thousands of race-loving tourists. The single-storeyed hotel does its year's trading in a day, or so it seems, and plane parking space on the bush airport is at a premium.

The Simpson Desert, like much of the arid inland, is not a featureless flat ocean of barrenness. Far from it. It is certainly dry and harsh but the desert landscape is constantly unfolding with new and different scenery. For example, botanists have identified eleven different sand-dune landscapes.

In the south, mazes of sand-dunes covered with nitre bush and sandhill cane grass are broken by dry river courses marked by coolibah trees. Permanent waterholes occur on the upper reaches of the rivers which drain to Lake Eyre. Water-dependent birds like budgerigars are common and camels and dingo tracks abound.

Here salt lakes, tiny versions of Lake Eyre, are surrounded by salt-tolerant plants like samphires. On higher ground woodlands of the inland acacia, gidgee wattle, grow in its gnarled and stunted form.

The Simpson Desert's greatest claim to fame is its pattern of sand-dunes. Thousands of dunes, all parallel, run for hundreds of kilometres in a NNW-SSE direction. Each dune is up to 200 kilometres long and up to 30 metres high. The shape of each dune is the same: a gentle slope of about 12 degrees on the western side and a steep 20-degree drop on the east. This makes driving four-wheel-drive vehicles from west to east possible and the reverse direction almost impossible.

The impression that a visitor gets of the Simpson Desert will largely depend on the length of time since the last rain. Shrubs will be rare after a prolonged drought or very thick soon after rain. As these shrub thickets reach the end of their normal life they die out and the desert reverts to a more open landscape. After a run of good seasons enough vegetation grows to support wild fires which may burn for hundreds of kilometres.

When rain does come to the desert, the ground is covered in tiny flowering plants. This brilliant display may last only a few weeks or months and the seeds produced lie dormant in the soil for years until the next rain.

One drought to the next

Droughts and the Australian outback go hand-in-hand. This has been a hard lesson for a developing nation to comprehend. The expectation that sheep and cattle grazing and wheat growing could prosper year after year and decade after decade came to a grinding halt at the turn of this century. Despite droughts in the 1860s and 1880s, it wasn't until the long so-called 'Federation' drought from 1895 to 1903 that the unreliability of Australia's climate finally struck home.

The noted Australian historian Geoffrey Blainey has suggested that Australia's prosperity to 1890 followed by the lean years can be significantly attributed to the fluctuations in climate of the time.

What is drought, and isn't the inland dry anyway? The normal dryness of the arid interior is usually no disaster. The plants, animals and Aboriginal inhabitants are well adapted to that. It is the time when only 5 per cent or less of the usual rainfall comes that the normal biological cycles cannot cope. It is this event that the weather scientists define as severe drought. This really doesn't tell the whole story, however, because very bad droughts occur when, for many months or even years, the same dry conditions continue.

The 'Federation' drought, which lasted seven years, affected large parts of the continent. It had an enormous impact on the attitude of Australians to drought since it brought the end to a series of boom periods that had continued since the first gold rushes. This drought halved the nation's sheep flock from about 100 million head in 1891 to 50 million in 1902. The cost in lost wool production in 1902 alone was close to £3 million.

But the effects of drought have even greater impact than the immediate economic ones. Since the land is now cultivated for pasture and grain production a new effect of drought is the widespread removal of topsoil from inland pastures. As the soil dries out, winds create dust storms which move tonnes of soil west to the coast. In the drought of the early 1980s spectacular dust storms swept through Sydney, Melbourne and Canberra. For the city-dwellers it was an inconvenience but to the farmers a permanent loss of topsoil and a permanent loss in long-term production. Disastrous bushfires are also often a consequence of long dry periods.

Long-term effects are also felt by native plants and animals. The death of large numbers of individual wild animals in droughts is a sad but normal part of life in an arid continent. With agricultural activities changing the normal patterns, the effects of drought on wildlife may now be permanent and not transitory.

To give an example. The bridled nail-tailed wallaby is a small kangaroo which was once widespread in western New South Wales and Queensland. It is now reduced to a tiny population living on one reserve in central Queensland. In the past, droughts would have killed large numbers of animals but small pockets would have survived to repopulate when wetter conditions returned. With the contraction in range of this rare wallaby because of competition with rabbits, predation by foxes and removal of scrub-lands, this species is now very vulnerable to the effects of future droughts.

Enormous research efforts have gone into trying to understand the causes of droughts. Scientists now have a good understanding of the underlying causes of the weather patterns which bring dry periods. Ultimately, the changing pattern of the temperature of the sea is the key to our understanding of droughts. However, in studies of Australia's major droughts of 1864, 1880, 1888, 1895, 1911, 1918, 1939, 1965, 1972 and 1982, all that we can be sure of is that another drought will come, but we don't know when.

The desert sea, Lake Eyre, is certainly no stranger to drought. This vast lake draining one side of the continent is usually a dry salt bed. Its surface is so hard that it was used in Campbell's 1964 record-breaking land speed record attempts. From 1894 to 1936 Lake Eyre received an average annual rainfall of 135 millimetres (or less than 6 inches). This makes it the driest place on the continent.

The 'rivers' which drain into the lake, Cooper Creek, the Diamantina and the Finke, are usually rocky creek beds. The water catchment of the lake includes three deserts: Sturt's Stony, Simpson and Strzelecki. But occasionally, about once a century, the lake fills. The 8800 square kilometres of salt pan and desert sands become a great lake and budgerigars and lizards make way for pelicans and fish. In 1974 and 1975 rains came and the lake filled to a level probably greater than any during European settlement. At its deepest point the water was over 6 metres and water flowed from Lake Eyre into the southern arm of the lake. Strings of islands were formed and a profusion of desert and wetland birds bred in numbers not witnessed before.

Now the lake has again become dry. The intense summer heat has evaporated the water and a crust of salt, metres thick, has formed on much of the lake surface. Four-wheel-drive vehicles have replaced boats for the scientists and tourists and the centre awaits the next inland deluge.

The mighty Murray and Darling rivers

Draining large parts of Victoria and New South Wales and parts of southern Queensland and South Australia, the Murray and Darling river system plays a variety of characters in the story of the inland. It was along the Murray that Sturt searched for the illusory 'inland sea' and this river became the boundary between the nation's most peopled States.

The largest river system in Australia played host to one of the most colourful periods in Australian history. In August 1853, with much fanfare, Captain Charles Francis Cadell R.N. steamed from Goolwa at the Murray River mouth in the *Lady Augusta*. On reaching the confluence with the Darling River, Captain Cadell won a prize from the South Australian government totalling about £3000. This prize had been established for the first steamer, of 40 horsepower and with a draught not exceeding 2 feet when loaded, to start trade along the river. Within forty years 140 steamers were plying the river system.

Inland trade was brisk. The boom agricultural years of the late 1800s saw wool, hides and timber carted to the railroads and supplies backloaded to the settlers' homes. The era of the paddlewheel and sternwheel steamers lasted only seventy years but not before a colourful new family of characters and tall stories became part of the Australian folklore.

When the *Eliza Jane* headed north from Goolwa on one trip she was not to return for three years. Near Bourke she ran out of water and a long dry spell saw her on dry land for fifteen months. Unperturbed, the boat captain and the crew turned to wood milling and, with the aid of a circular saw attached to the steam engine of the steamer, cut logs. Profit from the sawn timber was good and the steamer earned a profit as a lumber mill!

Steaming along the river today in the modern tourist steamers which are reviving the glory of past times, one could be forgiven for thinking that travel by steamer a century ago must have been an equal joy. One old-time captain, when quizzed on the apparent smallness of the cabins, joked they were especially designed that way to reduce the number of mosquitoes!

The steamboat era may have died but two legacies remain. The first is a series of locks and weirs used to maintain the depth of the river for the boats. In the lower Murray these locks are so close to one another that the river is essentially a series of ponds. The second is a tradition of river boating which is now being maintained by the increasing number of pleasure paddle-steamers, some new, some rebuilt, which now take tourists on nostalgic tours.

The river itself has been tamed and is no longer the glorious path it was. The weirs and locks, and now the large new water storage dams on the upper river, have controlled its most violent expression. No longer do floods spill out over thousands of kilometres of country or droughts reduce the river to puddles. The river red gums, Murray cod, waterfowl and other river life that depended on these cycles of feast or famine are now adjusting to a new regime.

Some will survive, others may not, but the character of the river plant and animal life has changed. Where once river red gums dominated the river banks, now introduced willows and poplars are found. Where huge fish like trout, cod, Macquarie perch and Murray cod were fished, now the exotic redfin, goldfish and carp are on the lines.

The quality of the water has also declined. It is now a drain for sewerage discharge, agricultural run-off waters containing fertilisers and pesticides, and industrial waste. It is said that each drop of the Murray's water passes through seven bladders before it reaches the sea. Maintaining the quality of the river's water is an administrative dilemma for the authorities involved. The river is the boundary of two States and a third, South Australia, essentially pays for any neglect. A fourth State, Queensland, has control of the important part of the headwaters.

Some of the first settlers of the inland were the squatters with their sheep and cattle. During the 1830s the wool industry expanded rapidly. At first they settled the major rivers like the Darling but later on even the most inhospitable country was settled. Setbacks occurred when international wool markets fluctuated and when labourers were lost during the great gold rushes from the 1850s on. Still, the national flock continued to grow, despite setbacks by droughts, disease and depredations by dingoes. Kinchega, now a national park, was one of the first large runs west of the Darling River. By 1876 the property had accommodation for forty shearers and had a vast shearing shed, with twenty-six stands, which can still be seen today.

Breeds of sheep especially suited for the dry harsh interior were developed by George Peppin on his properties in the Riverina. Wool was carted from inland properties by bullock dray or river paddle-steamer. Later in the 1800s the railways hauled the wool to the ports. Fast ocean clippers took the Australian wool to the markets of Europe.

Hand-operated shears were the rule of the day until 1885 when Fred Wolsely invented a shearing machine. By the beginning of the twentieth century mechanical shears had replaced hand shears. Shearing is backbreaking work and has developed its own place in the folklore and traditions of the nation. Good shearers can shear 250 sheep in a working day and the record is held by Bill Robertson who shore 421 merinos in a working day of 7 hours and 48 minutes.

At the turn of the century Sir Walter Merriman developed strains of merinos which produce superfine wool. Yass, near present-day Canberra, is now the centre of the world's superfine wool regions. Today's national sheep flock stands at about 150 million and cattle numbers are over 20 million.

Perhaps the most colourful of the earliest immigrants to arid inland Australia were the so-called 'Afghans'. They came from what is now Pakistan but the name of Afghan stuck. They came to Australia in charge of the large number of camels brought in as transport animals for the desert areas. They remained to work the camels under some of the hardest conditions in the world. Camels were able to work in country too dry for horses and bullocks, country which did not produce grazing on which other animals could live. Their other great advantages were that they could work for years on end without being spelled and their feet were incredibly tough and able to withstand the harshest terrain.

There were, of course, drawbacks to the carriage of goods by camel. As they were pack animals they had to be unloaded at night and loaded again the next day. However, there were some cases in which they were broken in to work as teams pulling wagons.

The Afghans and their camels were a familiar sight at all the remote railheads in Australia working to take the freight on to outlying mines and sheep stations. It seems only right therefore that the air-conditioned train that takes droves of tourists from Adelaide to Alice Springs should be called 'The Ghan'.

For those requiring more of the creature comforts when travelling no name is more evocative of the romance of the Australian outback than that of Cobb & Co.

Freeman Cobb, a young American, arrived in Melbourne in the gold-rush days of the early 1850s when that city was booming and thousands of men were clamouring to get to the diggings as quickly as possible. Many were forced to walk the 160 kilometres or so pushing barrows loaded with their mining gear.

Cobb came out to Australia originally as the employee of an American carrying business but by the end of 1853 he and three other young Americans had established Cobb & Co. It was a very expensive operation to establish at that time because men and horses were scarce and coaches and harness had to be imported from America. There was also the need to establish changing stations with stables along the coach routes and also to arrange for places where hungry travellers would be fed.

However, in the Melbourne *Argus* of 30 January 1854 the energetic Cobb and his partners announced that their 'well appointed coaches' would run a daily service from Melbourne to Forest Creek and Bendigo. Every attention was promised to ensure punctuality. On the dot of 6 a.m. on that day the first coach dashed away from the Criterion Hotel in Collins Street and Cobb & Co. became a household name to all Australians until 1924 when it yielded to the train, plane and motor vehicle.

The first Cobb & Co. coach was the Concord Jack type which had an egg-shaped body suspended on leather braces. Inside in crimson plush splendour rode nine passengers and up to five passengers were carried outside. The body was red and the wheels and undercarriage yellow. To our hardy forebears it was the epitome of luxury travel. With eight spirited horses and a whip-cracking driver the Concord Jack must have made a splendid sight on that summer morning in Melbourne.

To make good its claim to punctuality, Cobb & Co. used none but the finest horses and these were changed every 16 kilometres. The roads were so bad that at times they had to be closed but Cobb & Co. would make the 145 kilometres to Bendigo in a day which was regarded as a remarkable performance at that time.

Cobb and his partners, go-getting young Americans that they were, stayed in the business only a couple of years and Cobb then returned to the United States. He became a senator but in the 1870s he was engaged in coaching in South Africa.

The name of Cobb & Co. was not abandoned and soon it was to be seen on coaches in all the eastern States of Australia. Under pressure from the advancing railways the coaches pushed further out into the pastoral districts providing the only transport link to remote mining areas and the scattered homes of pioneer sheep and cattle stations. Cobb & Co. coaches were as familiar in the tropical jungle of northern Queensland as they were in the high snow country around Mount Kosciusko.

In the main the Australian trains which forced the Cobb & Co. coaches from the scene were rather dull machines by comparison. On the whole they lacked the romance attached to train travel on other continents. But an Australian train and track which does appeal to the imagination is the transcontinental joining Sydney and Perth. The total journey on the Indian-Pacific is 3961 kilometres and takes five days and three nights. A line linking the two sides of the country was completed in 1917. However, this was not built to a standard gauge. It was not until 1970 that a standard gauge line, 1.41 metres wide, allowed passengers to travel from the Indian Ocean to the Pacific Ocean in the same train. The world's longest straight stretch of railway line, 478 kilometres, is on the Nullarbor Plain section of the track.

The Royal Flying Doctor Service

In 1928 the Australian arid outback became a little smaller and a lot safer. In that year a remarkable Australian, John Flynn, established the Australian Inland Mission Aerial Medical Service at Cloncurry in western Queensland.

The company which provided the plane for the service to start was Queensland and Northern Territory Aerial Services. The flying medical service went on to become the Royal Flying Doctor Service and the airline, Qantas. The original concept of the service was quite simple. Remote locations were provided with a simple portable radio transceiver and a basic medical kit. A radio message could bring the outpost in contact with a doctor 24 hours a day. Depending on the situation a doctor could be flown to the patient in a matter of hours, the patient could be evacuated to a hospital or treatment could be prescribed from the medical kit. The concept was to provide a 'mantle of safety' for the people of the outback.

Today the service has grown but is still based on the original concepts. Over 100 000 consultations are handled around Australia annually. About thirty aircraft are involved across the continent and about 8000 aerial evacuations are completed each year. The Royal Flying Doctor Service is now a non-denominational service that provides care without regard to the ability to pay for its services.

The radio network which runs the Royal Flying Doctor Service is also used to conduct the School of the Air. For isolated primary school children, the School of the Air is a supplement to their correspondence classes. Throughout Australia more than 1200 students tune into the School of the Air each school day.

Not all of Australia's best known inhabitants of the harsh outback were so philanthrophic and some were quite notorious. Thus, even now, if the average Australian is asked to name the most famous person in Australian nineteenth-century history he is just as likely to say 'Ned Kelly'.

It is not surprising that for many years the pastoral districts of the Australian colonies were ravaged by bushrangers. From the earliest days convicts escaped from the chain-gangs into the bush and they were made more bloodthirsty and desperate by the certain knowledge that death would be swift if they were captured.

The notorious bushranger Ned Kelly was hanged in Melbourne gaol in 1880 and has become the Australian byword for courage. His old mother who was also an inmate in the gaol at the time of the hanging said to him 'mind you die like a Kelly, Ned!' and his last words were 'such is life'.

The Kelly gang's most notorious raid was the capture of the small Riverina town of Jerilderie in 1879. The gang of four first captured the two police officers in their station at midnight on a Saturday night. Next day, dressed in police uniforms, they reconnoitred the town, taking one of their police captives to show them around. On the Monday the outlaws struck, rounding up in the hotel all those whom they felt might resist them. They then robbed the Bank of New South Wales of about £200 had a few leisurely drinks with their captives and rode off to their Victorian lair. The governments of New South Wales and Victoria put a price of £2000 on the head of each of the outlaws. In the following year the Kelly gang captured the small town of Glenrowan in north-eastern Victoria and, expecting a police contingent to come from Melbourne when the news got out, they took up a large piece of track to wreck the train. The gang waited in the hotel, drinking with the captives, but one of them escaped in time to give a danger signal to the approaching train. The gang was finally cornered in the Glenrowan Hotel where three of them died. Ned Kelly came out in his famous iron helmet and body armour but was wounded and captured.

Opal mining

To this day, life in the inland continues to be hard. Of all those working in this tough environment, inland Australia's opal miners are probably the best adapted. Australia produces about 90 per cent of the world's opals from six main mining areas, all of which are found in the arid inland. The most productive mining area is Coober Pedy in South Australia and the best known mine areas in New South Wales are White Cliffs and Lightning Ridge. Australia is the main world supplier of opals, the main markets being in Hong Kong, Japan and the United States.

Opals are semiprecious gemstones which when polished make fine jewellery. Its value is partly determined by its colour and the so-called black opal is the most valuable. The world's most valuable opal was mined at Coober Pedy in 1956 and is said to be worth $1.8 million.

Opals are found in wide-ranging fields and mining cannot be profitably mechanised. As a consequence the industry has remained on a small scale with each miner digging his own claim. Opal clay is examined on the surface and a shaft dug down to exploit it. Shafts of up to 30 metres are as deep as opal miners usually work.

Opal miners are a tough breed living in a scorching climate. Most residences in Coober Pedy are built underground to avoid the surface heat. Many of these underground dwellings are quite sophisticated with several rooms, 'wall-mounted cupboards' and other fittings dug into the walls.

Prospectors were first encouraged to the inland with the building of the overland telegraph from Adelaide to Darwin. It was a great technological achievement, all the more praiseworthy because of the country through which the line passed. It was also a feat of great personal endurance for the teams working on the line. The 5000 kilometres of line across some of the driest parts of the continent connected Australia to the world in 1872. Darwin had been connected by undersea cables to Java and, eventually, London the previous year.

Despite the incalculable effects of having instant communication with the rest of the world, the overland telegraph brought little financial reward. Other undersea cables reached other Australian centres and the inland line lost much of its financial importance.

However, the importance of the line to the development of the Red Centre was very significant. The telegraph stations scattered along the route were used as staging posts for further inland exploration. Prospectors and pastoralists followed. The most famous centre to develop as a consequence of the line was Alice Springs. The springs on the Todd River were named after the wife of Charles Todd, the superintendent of the construction of the telegraph line. Located at a break in the MacDonnell Ranges, Alice Springs rapidly became a supply centre for much of central Australia.

The Alice

The town at Alice Springs was originally named Stuart after the famous inland explorer. In 1933 the town's name was changed to that of its famous springs. The town at the heart of Australia is now part of the world of the jet set. Boasting an international airport, casino and international five-star hotels, 'The Alice' is now very little like Nevil Shute's *A Town Like Alice*. The Alice is now a thriving tourist centre in its own right.

The rugged inland ranges, which posed such a problem to early travellers, are now viewed, sometimes from hot air balloons, with awe and amazement. The memorials to John Flynn and builders of the telegraph line are meccas to tourists as are the museums and shops displaying and selling Aboriginal artefacts.

But the real inland centre is a half-day's drive away at Ayers Rock, Uluru. The great red rock is now a symbol to all Australians of the vastness, beauty and traditions of the outback.

Uluru and Kata Tjuta (or the Olgas as Europeans know them) are part of Uluru National Park. On the edge of the park the town of Yulara sits nestled among the sanddunes. With its international airport, five-star hotel and architect-designed buildings it looks more like a science fiction movie set than an inland town.

Here, sheltered from the harsh desert outside, the tourist can enjoy all the home comforts and make forays into the park. What would the old-timers say!

To Europeans, Uluru is the tip of a vast unbroken sandstone block which disappears into the earth for over 6 kilometres. It is the remnant of rocks which formed beneath a sea 600 million years ago. The parallel lines which come across the rock are the layers of deposited sand which are now lying at right angles to their original position. The thirty-six rock domes which make up Kata Tjuta (the Olgas) have been formed from the same sandstone formations.

To Aborigines Uluru and Kata Tjuta are parts of the landscape created by their ancestral beings. Before the Dreamtime the land was flat and featureless. As the ancestral beings crossed over the land, they created the features, both living and inanimate, that we see today. At each of these sites the events that took place are recountable. Most of the ancestral trails within Uluru National Park start and finish in places a long way further off in the inland deserts. The wide travels of the ancestral beings therefore link Aboriginal peoples from a wide area.

As well, Uluru links two races and is an inland Dreamtime place for two cultures.

Remnant of an ancient plateau, Chambers Pillar, south of Alice Springs, rises 34 metres above the plain like an old carved column standing on a giant pedestal.

Ayers Rock, the largest rock in the world, is about 8 kilometres in circumference and rises abruptly out of the red desert to a height of 350 metres. (Previous page.)

Sunset intensifies the rich red ochre hue of Ayers Rock in central Australia. Huge primitive, old as time, Ayers Rock has an atmosphere of eerie splendour and to the Aborigines it is a major element of the great Dreamtime stories. (Page 97.)

Ormiston Gorge, reflected in the still waters of the Finke River. The most colourful of all Australian gorges, Ormiston has wildly fractured orange and red quartzite walls.

A grove of luxurious Livistonia mariae *at Palm Valley in the Finke Gorge National Park, Northern Territory. One of the rarest trees in the world, this relict tropical palm's continued existence in the heat of the Australian desert is due to microclimates provided along the Finke River Gorge system.*

Lizard Rock, a strangely shaped rock formation found in the MacDonnell Ranges in the centre of the continent.

Rows of sugarcane near Prosperine in the heart of Queensland's cane country.

Towering more than 70 metres high, the sheer walls of Standley Chasm in the Northern Territory are of bright orange quartzite which contrasts strikingly with the white pebbled floor.◄

The Glasshouse Mountains, Queensland – an intriguing mixture of narrow spires and massive rounded bluffs. (Following page.)

The Norman River winds sluggishly over the tidal flats of northern Queensland inscribing intricate patterns of blue water, brown mud and green mangroves.

Shallow falls on the Leichhardt River in north-western Queensland.

Millstream Falls—Australia's widest waterfall—situated in woodlands on the eastern slope of the Atherton Tableland, near Ravenshoe, Queensland.▼

The Atherton Tableland in Queensland was once almost entirely covered with rainforest but it is now mostly cleared and dotted with farmhouses.

Pisonia trees (Pisonia grandis) *provide soft leafy vegetation on cays on the Great Barrier Reef.*▼

Stretching into the horizon, massed golden wildflowers border a road in outback New South Wales.

Rural scene in the Hunter Valley, New South Wales, Australia's oldest commercial wine producing area.

Flood plains dotted with occasional trees near Tibooburra in the arid inland regions of New South Wales. (Following page.)

The Breadknife—a narrow wall towering 100 metres above the valley in the Warrumbungles, New South Wales.

Wentworth Falls, one of the many magnificent scenic attractions in the Blue Mountains, New South Wales.

Vibrant wildflowers border a rock-strewn creek in a pretty corner of the Tarra Valley National Park in South Gippsland, Victoria.➤

The massive sandstone ranges of the Grampians, which rise to over 1000 metres in western Victoria, provide some of the State's most spectacular scenery. (Following page.)

Myall Lakes—a place of peace and solitude in the centre of the busy eastern coast of New South Wales.

Sparkling sunrise on the Goulburn River, Alexandra, Victoria.▸

Sheer and rocky, Mount Sturgeon is one of the many superbly sculptured formations in the Grampians, Victoria. ◂

River gums line the banks of the Murray River at Echuca, Victoria. ▾

Buffalo Dam, near Myrtleford in the Ovens Valley, Victoria. Nestled in the foothills of the Victorian Alps, the Ovens Valley was opened up by miners flocking to the area, and the local creeks are still popular for gold panning and gem fossicking.

Snow blankets Lake Catani on Mount Buffalo, Victoria. In milder weather, camping is popular on the shores of this picturesque lake.

Surrounded by mountains, the man-made Lake Pedder reflects the many moods of nature in the south-western wilderness of Tasmania.

Ben Lomond's lofty plateau, with its precipitous sides, is the highest region of north-eastern Tasmania and the state's premier snow sports area. ◄

Cave interiors on the state reserves in Tasmania are dramatically lit to enhance the wonderland of limestone-derived calcite formations.

One of the four crater lakes at Mount Gambier, South Australia, an extinct volcano in the centre of the largest pine plantations in the country.

The notorious Birdsville Track, near Marree, South Australia. The track starts at Marree, once a supply outpost for the Afghan camel traders, and follows the route originally used to drove cattle from south-western Queensland to the railhead at Marree.

The Murray River winds through farmland near Swan Reach, South Australia. Through its tributaries, which originate in four states, the Murray drains about one-sixth of the Australian continent.

A wall of precipitous peaks encloses the oval-shaped Wilpena Pound, probably the best known part of the Flinders Ranges in South Australia. The Aboriginal word 'Wilpena' means 'place of bent fingers' and is thought to relate to the pound's resemblance to a cupped hand. ▲

The enormous salt Lake Eyre, South Australia, has been filled only twice since white men first reached the desert. ◄

Tranquil Lake Argyle in Western Australia was created by the Ord River Scheme. Covering more than 700 square kilometres, it contains nine times as much water as Sydney Harbour and teems with wildlife. (Following page.)

The fertile Fleurieu Peninsula, south of Adelaide. ►

The Hamersley Range in Western Australia is one of the largest iron ore provinces in the world and a major economic resource of Australia. The range is rugged, forbidding country, basically broad and flat, relieved only by low residual ridges and hummocky hills.

Cut by the big Fitzroy River at the junction of the Oscar and Geikie ranges, Geikie Gorge in Western Australia has beautifully sculptured cliffs, lush riverine vegetation and deep permanent waters.

The settlement of Kununurra, Western Australia, built to service the Ord River Scheme, became the only new town to be established in the Kimberleys this century.

Thousands of mysterious limestone pinnacles are scattered over the gently undulating desert landscape of Nambung National Park in Western Australia.

The Murchison River has eroded into coastal sandstone in Kalbarri National Park, Western Australia. Usually a chain of long, still pools, this river flows only occasionally after heavy rains when it becomes a muddy brown torrent. (Following page.)

The man-made Lake Argyle nestles in the ancient massive rock plateau of the Kimberleys in Western Australia.

THE FLOWERS AND TREES

Most of Australia's flowering trees are evergreen, which immediately separates them from the deciduous flowering trees of the Northern Hemisphere. In fact, Australia's forests and bushlands are dominated by members of two evergreen groups: the acacias and the eucalypts. Australia's plants have a strong similarity to the species dominant in South Africa and South America. For example, the southern continents are the centre of distribution for the proteas which include the Australian grevilleas, waratahs and banksias.

The deserts of Australia are the most diverse arid lands in the Southern Hemisphere. The plants found here contain a blend of ancient Australian stock combined with recent, geologically speaking, cosmopolitan species. There are few succulent species like cactus and most Australian arid plants have a range of techniques to withstand severe dehydration. Many desert species survive arid times as seed and only grow and flower following rain.

Australia's alpine flora, despite being restricted in area, carry a rare combination of ancient Southern Hemisphere plants and adapted modern ones.

Otherwise, the antipodean flora are dominated by the hard-leaved shrubs and trees typical of the poor soils of the south-east and south-west. The seasonal flowering of these highly diverse plant communities appealed to the first botanists as it does to thousands of tourists today.

The strange 'bush', as Australian forests are known, of the new continent was, to most of the first settlers, a major obstacle to be cleared away to make way for food-producing crops. Most of the first clearings around Sydney, however, produced very little food and became ugly 'bad lands'. Fortunately for the hungry colony fertile land was soon discovered at Parramatta and good crops were able to grow. However, the perception of the bush being a worthless obstacle has unfortunately become embedded in the national psyche. Many Australians still look to European or tropical landscapes to find beauty in plants. It is encouraging that at least one First Fleeter perceived the natural beauty of the flora of his new home. Captain Tench observed that

a variety of flowering shrubs abound, most of them entirely new to a European, and surpassing in beauty, fragrance and number, all I ever saw in an uncultivated state...[these] deserve the highest admiration and panegyric.

Gondwanaland

To understand the reasons for the appearance of the plant life of Australia it is useful to look back to the world as it was 200 million years ago. Then, South America, Africa, India, Antarctica and Australia were one vast continent. This continent of Gondwanaland began to break up around 110 million years ago by a process known as continental drift. As Australia moved slowly northward and the continent became more arid many of the original plants adapted to the new conditions. But many plants whose origins were in the cool, wet landmass of Gondwanaland continue to survive only in the moist areas of south-eastern Australia and Tasmania. Related plants can still be found in modern South America, South Africa and New Zealand. Their fossils are now found beneath the Antarctic ice.

The famous biologist Charles Darwin remarked in 1859 on the similarity

between the flora of the south-western corner of Australia and the Cape of Good Hope...this will, no doubt, some day be explained.

It took over a century for the theory of continental drift to be proposed and supported before Darwin's explanation was found.

Typical of the ancient Gondwanaland plants is the magnificent huon pine which grows in the cold and wet river basins of western Tasmania. The huon pine has long been a highly sought-after timber tree and has been used for boat building and other specialist joinery purposes.

Huon pines can grow to 35 metres in height and a metre in diameter. Unfortunately huon pines are now very scarce both from previous logging and from the flooding of some rivers in dam construction.

What happened to Australia's plant life as the continent began moving towards the Equator about 110 million years ago?

At first, vast rainforests continued to cover the continent. Huon pines have been recorded in fossil deposits throughout Australia's current deserts. Slowly, as the rainfall became more erratic, new drier vegetation types increased in number. These were the eucalypts, wattles, casuarinas and callitris pines. Fire became an important factor in the spread of plant species and the incidence of fire increased with the arrival of Aborigines up to 100 000 years ago. The fire-sensitive species such as casuarinas and callitris pines were confined, and the fire-tolerant species like eucalypts and wattles spread more rapidly. Fire also continued to limit the spread of rainforest species in all parts of the country.

Plants species do not occur at random. Plants are usually found growing together in communities. These are given names such as rainforest, open forest, woodland and heath.

In Australia, rainforests occur in high-rainfall coastal parts of Queensland, New South Wales and western Tasmania. Rainforests are places of extraordinary plant richness. In the rainforest of the Atherton Tableland in northern Queensland, 164 different tree species were recorded in a plot 30 metres square. The northern rainforests are also rich in vines and large buttressed trees. About 75 per cent of all Australia's rainforests have been cleared. Animal production, sugarcane, bananas and potatoes are the main crops. One large area of rainforest around Lismore in New South Wales was known to the first settlers as the 'Big Scrub'. Less than half a per cent of the 750 square kilometres of that forest remains today.

The most common Australian forest types are the open forests so typical of much of the eastern coast from Cape York to Melbourne. Tall eucalypts dominate. These forests are subject to frequent summer fires. It was one of these coastal eucalypt forests that the early Polish botanist John Lhotsky said was of 'mind blunting monotony'. Even the great and perceptive biologist Charles Darwin said that the long strands of eucalypt bark gave the woods 'a desolate and untidy appearance'.

Darwin had been away from his native English home for four years and could perhaps have been forgiven his homesickness. These forests contain some of this country's most beautiful and most valuable trees such as the mountain ash of Victoria and the jarrah in Western Australia.

Other major vegetation communities include the woodlands, which have been largely taken over by sheep and wheat farms. These are areas of greatest eucalypt variety and where many native tussock grasses are to be found. The low bush country of much of Australia's inland is diverse in its plant life despite its apparent sameness.

Of surprise to many people is that much of the inland is in fact well covered in plants including extensive woodlands and shrublands. The species found in these areas include a variety of eucalypts, native pines and mulga. Some of the shrublands are of great importance for pastoral activities. About 6 per cent of the continent is bluebush and saltbush shrubland and this supports more than 2.5 million sheep.

Two of the major threats to the continued survival of many of these distinctive Australian arid land communities are the depredations of the introduced rabbit and agricultural mismanagement.

The impression many people have of inland Australia is a vast open country covered in grasses and herbs. This is usually the exception, although areas of grasslands do occur in the north, from the Kimberleys to the Barkly Tableland. These plains are covered in Mitchell grass which forms the basis of the northern pastoral industries.

Eucalypts, or gum trees as they are usually known, are some of the most visible of

Australia's plants. The eucalypts form the dominant forest tree in about a third of the country. They are a uniquely Australasian plant. Six hundred different species are known and they grow naturally only in Australia and New Guinea and some nearby islands. Curiously, no eucalypts are known in New Zealand or the islands of the south-west Pacific.

The word eucalypt comes from the Greek words for 'well covered' and refers to the little lids that cover the emerging flowers. If it wasn't for these lids the famous May Gibbs storybook characters, Snugglepot and Cuddlepie, wouldn't have hats to wear!

Eucalypts are evergreen plants which are usually trees and many are quite large. The tallest is the mountain ash of Victoria and Tasmania. Trees of 100 metres in height are known. The mountain ash is exceeded in height only by the redwoods of California, which are the tallest trees in the world. Other massive trees include the Western Australian karri and the flooded gum of New South Wales, which both reach about 70 metres in height. Some species such as the narrow-leafed Sally, found in the Blue Mountains are hardly more than shrubs.

About forty species of eucalypts have an unusual and highly distinctive growth form. These are the mallees. They do not have a single trunk but many trunks emerging from the ground. Some eucalypts grow only in the mallee shape; some species which are usually well-formed trees will grow in the mallee shape on infertile sites. Several inland eucalypts which grow in the mallee shape are so widespread that the name mallee now also refers to this type of low inland forest.

One of the remarkable features of the eucalypts is the amazing sameness of the adult leaves of the hundreds of species. They generally have even-coloured, long and downward-hanging leaves. Many species have contrasting juvenile leaves that have features which are useful to the botanist in classifying the various types.

Not all of the eucalypt's leaf buds are used as the tree grows. Some remain concealed in the branches and trunk. When the tree is under stress, such as in drought, after fire, during insect attack or after pruning, the tree is then able to send out new shoots from the trunk and branches.

Eucalypts have developed strategies to withstand droughts which are unlike the methods used by dry-country plants in other continents such as the cactuses. Eucalypts have wide-ranging roots which are highly efficient at finding water. They have hard tissues in the stems and leaves which stop wilting. In the tropics some eucalypts even lose their leaves as the Dry Season progresses.

The eucalypts are also well adapted to survive the inevitable fires of the Australian bush. The bark on most eucalypts is very thick and provides good insulation for the deeper living tissues. Most large trees are not killed in a fire even when all the leaves and smaller branches are removed and the bark is totally blackened. The new leaf buds will soon emerge from the bark and branches. In a less severe fire the leaves may be merely replaced. In a still less severe fire adult trees may survive totally unscathed and only the young seedlings will be killed.

Some trees have adapted to release large amounts of seed immediately after a fire. The seedlings have a great opportunity to get started in the ash-bed, without competition from other plants. This strategy is usually used by eucalypts which are more susceptible to fire damage as adults.

Eucalypts are now the most widely planted tree in the world. With shortages in timber for paper production, sawlogs, domestic fires and construction the merits of eucalypts for a wide range of uses and sites are now recognised. One of the many hundreds of eucalypt species can usually be found to match special overseas requirements. A limiting factor is that eucalypts will not grow in places where the soil freezes. This essentially limits the Northern Hemisphere cultivated range at about 45 degrees of latitude and this excludes places such as northern Europe, Canada and northern China.

In parts of Australia large numbers of eucalypts are dying. This is usually given the name 'dieback' and is not a single disease condition but refers to a wide range of problems. One cause of large-scale death of trees is root fungus. The fungus becomes established in an area of forest and, when the soil is wet and warm, can spread quickly. Large areas of jarrah forest in Western Australia and thousands of hectares of silver-topped ash in Victoria are affected. The root fungus lives in the soil and is spread by construction and forestry equipment.

A different problem causes the death of eucalypts in farmlands. Although it too is called 'dieback' it is caused by a range of factors, not just one. One area particularly devastated in recent decades is the northern tablelands of New South Wales based around Armidale although trees in many farming areas face the same threats.

Agricultural practices change the nature of the soil. The watertable may drop, fertility changes with the addition of fertilisers, and the structure of the soil changes with the coming of hard-hooved domestic animals like sheep and cattle. In many areas, most trees were removed by ringbarking at the turn of this century. This practice often left only older shade trees. The dieback that is now occurring is caused by a suite of factors. The over-mature trees are dying and the domestic stock are stopping the growth of new trees. Some trees are dying through the combined effects of lowered watertable and drought. Others succumb to the pressures of leaf-eating insects which are now concentrated on fewer trees. In many parts of rural Australia the appearance of landscape is changing, probably permanently, as a consequence of agricultural practices of the last century.

Acacias

Acacias, or wattles as we know them in Australia, occur throughout the world. However, Australia has over 700 species, which is more than half the known species, and so they are often identified with Australian landscapes. The Australian bush, except for the true rainforests and the most arid deserts, is dominated by the acacias or eucalypts and sometimes both.

Overseas, the flowers of acacias are known as mimosa. However, from the very earliest days in the Australian colonies these showy plants were called 'wattles'. It is commonly believed that this came from the technique for constructing rough huts consisting of cutting bundles of sticks and sealing them into the walls with mud. The plants commonly used for this purpose were the acacias. On the other hand, some early settlers report that some Aborginal tribes called the acacia 'wattah'. Was this a true Aboriginal name and did the name wattle derive from this, or had the Aboriginal tribes already adopted a European name?

All acacia flowers are yellow or pale cream. The differences between the species centre on the leaves, the arrangement of flowers and the form of the plant.

Some acacias have leaves like ferns. One of the first Australian plants ever described was an acacia of this type which was collected by a Dutchman on the Swan River in 1697. The Dutch botanist Burman, lacking the flowers and having just a sample of the leaves, described this acacia as a fern! Most acacias have large, flat 'leaves' which are in fact not leaves at all but highly modified leafstalks. This is hard to believe until you find an occasional 'leaf' with a proper ferny leaf growing from its top. This is a most strange sight. In some acacias even these false leaves are absent or reduced to sharp spines. The flowers on acacias are usually scattered along a branch among the leaves or bundled in large showy clusters at the ends of the branches like the famous Mudgee or golden wattles.

The acacias have a variety of shapes. Some are low ground-hugging shrubs a few centimetres high and many are lofty rainforest trees, such as the Tasmanian blackwood, a fine timber species.

One of the most spectacular of all the acacias is the Cootamundra wattle. Found naturally only around the country town of southern New South Wales with which it shares its name, the Cootamundra wattle has rather sombre blue-grey leaves. However, come August, the brilliant show of yellow flowers covers the tree. It is now widely grown in gardens throughout southern Australia. Unfortunately this tree is relatively short-lived, about fifteen years, and because of this, all acacias now have the same undeserved reputation.

Banksias

Banksias are an exclusively Australian plant. They have large showy flowers which are particularly attractive to pollen-feeding birds and small mammals. About fifty different species are known and the greatest concentration is in the south-western corner of Western Australia.

Banksias were named in honour of the famous English botanist and patron Sir Joseph Banks. History has bestowed the honour of 'father of Australian botany' on this man who accompanied Cook on his 1770 voyage of discovery to Australia's eastern coast.

Banks was fortunate to be born into the great age of the 'Gentlemen amateur'. He was independently wealthy and had a passion for botany and studied at Harrow, Eton and Oxford. At the age of twenty-five he was able to use his social connections and financial resources to have himself, and eight others, given permission to join Cook's expedition to the South Seas. The *Endeavour* set sail on 25 August 1768 and did not return for almost three years. During that time Banks and his colleague Daniel Solander collected 3000 botanical specimens including 1300 new species. All these specimens are now held by the Natural History Museum in London. When the famous Swedish naturalist Linnaeus formally described some of the plants in Banks' collection he named the banksias in his honour.

For four months in 1770 Banks, Solander and their staff collected and drew hundreds of plant specimens along the Australian east coast. Cook named Botany Bay because of

the great quantity of plants Mr Banks and Mr Solander found in this place!

It is a little ironic that the paper that Banks used to dry the plant specimens at Botany Bay were taken from volumes of Milton's *Paradise Lost*. This wealth of plants has now, years later, certainly disappeared under suburban Sydney.

Banksias belong to the large protea family. The family is centred on southern Africa and Australia and probably prompted Charles Darwin's comments relating the plant life of the two areas. The protea family includes such well-known plants as the grevilleas and waratahs.

The banksias are usually shrubs or bushes but some are ground-hugging creepers and one, the Western Australian river banksia, grows into a tree 15 metres high. A feature of this group of plants is the gnarled, twisted appearance of the trunks and branches of mature specimens. The flower spikes have a striking appearance. Growing directly from a branch the flower bloom is usually shaped like a cylinder with large numbers of individual flowers tightly packed together. After the flower dies the woody cone remains. The cones are often used for decorative purposes and have given rise to the 'banksia men' of Australian children's storybooks.

Banksias have developed a number of strategies for surviving the fires which regularly sweep through the coastal forests and heathlands. In some species such as the heath-leafed banksia the entire plant is killed by the fire and a large amount of seed is produced from the many seed-bearing cones which open on the dead plant. The seed is released onto the fire ash-bed and, without competition from other plants, becomes established quickly. In these species it is critical that the next fire does not come until the new plants are old enough to have produced some seed. This may be many years. The fern-leafed banksia survives fire by a combination of seed spread after the fire and by sending shoots from the surviving underground stems. The final strategy for surviving fire is demonstrated by the wallum banksia which has very thick bark. The centre of the trunk is not killed by the fire and new shoots appear on the trunk and branches.

Native orchids

The native orchids can be divided into two obvious groups. The first are the epiphytes, which are those that grow on trees or rocks. The second group are the terrestrial orchids, which grow only in the ground. The Australian epiphytic orchids are found only on the eastern coast in the wetter eucalypt forests and rainforests. The most spectacular of these orchids is the State flower of Queensland, the Cooktown orchid. By far the largest group of Australian orchids are the generally smaller terrestrial species. They range in size from the tiny mosquito orchids to the large swamp orchids of coastal Queensland which has a flower stalk up to 2 metres high and the largest flower of any Australian orchid.

Curiously, the extraordinary plants of Australia have never seemed to evoke the same incredulity as some of the continent's animals. Two plants which must set the record straight are the underground orchids. These orchids are unlikely to win a flower show with their tiny flowers but are remarkable in that they grow and flower underground! Two species of these subterranean orchids are known: one from a few localities from Brisbane to the Blue Mountains, near Sydney, and the other from south-western Western Australia.

The underground orchids live on a fungus which grows on the roots of certain gum trees and broom-bushes. The flowers are probably pollinated by small ants, termites and beetles which are attracted to its strong smell. Once the seed is produced it is pushed to the surface to be dispersed.

Recent research in southern Australia has revealed a fascinating relationship between Australian native plants and birds. Many bird species are adapted to feed on nectar from flowers and for many years it has been known that birds, particularly honeyeaters, contributed to the pollination of flowers. Pollination is usually done by the plants themselves or by insects. However, it was not realised how significant birds were and how many plants depended on birds as pollinators. In south-western Western Australia over 600 species of plants depend on birds as the primary pollinators of their flowers. These include many of the banksias, kangaroo-paws, bottlebrushes, grevilleas and honeyflowers.

As a consequence, the flowers of these plants are adapted to attract birds not insects. Since birds have no sense of smell other features are needed to attract them. Bird-attracting flowers are predominantly red in colour but yellow and white are also important. The most common flower is bowl-shaped like the eucalypts. Somehow birds are able to detect which plants are producing the most nectar and concentrate their feeding on these. It appears that the plants which are able to attract the greatest number of birds are liable to be the most successful and produce more seed. Many marsupials are now also being recognised as having an important pollinating role and these include the tiny honey possum, feather-tailed glider and pygmy possums.

Floral emblems

Flowers have long been used as symbols. The significance of many plants such as ivy, hawthorn and palms goes back to the folklore and religious beliefs of the European ancestors of most Australians.

It is only natural that Australians should seek to identify with the native plants of their country and use them as symbols. Native flowers form a natural living heritage with links through botanical history to the first European exploration of the continent.

Although the golden wattle enjoys the status of being Australia's national floral emblem it is without any official declaration. This wattle appears as the background for the national Coat of Arms. The designs of the insignia of the Order of Australia are based on an individual ball of wattle flowers. Australian sportsmen and women always wear gold and green which is claimed to be based on the colours of the golden wattle. Thus by default rather than official patronage the golden wattle is Australia's national floral emblem.

Golden wattle grows as a small tree up to 8 metres in height. It is found in open woodlands in South Australia, Victoria, New South Wales and the Australian Capital Territory. It is a resilient plant which reproduces vigorously after fire. This wattle grows well in cultivation and has been widely planted overseas.

The floral emblem for New South Wales is the waratah. The brilliant red flowers appear in the bush near Sydney in spring and early summer. The scientific name is based on Greek words meaning 'beautiful handsome plant seen from afar'. The flowers are really quite magnificent but the shrub is rather disappointing. The rank woody shrub appears not to truly compliment such beautiful blooms. The waratah grows only in the infertile sandstone soils in the immediate vicinity of Sydney.

An interesting story concerning the selection of the national and New South Wales floral emblems throws some light on the rivalry between Australia's two most populous States. Although the arguments could be debated at length, the brilliant red flower of the waratah is probably a stronger and more attractive symbol than the paler, more open wattle bloom. The waratah also belongs to a group of plants which are found only in Australia. Wattles on the other hand grow in many other parts of the world. However, waratahs don't grow in Victoria and the golden wattle grows in both States. This has settled the matter. The conflict has been so great that the official shovels used by the Govenor-General and his party at the launching of Canberra in 1913 were decorated with two floral blooms: the waratah and the golden wattle!

Victoria's floral emblem, the common heath, grows in Victoria, of course, and neighbouring States. The common heath has a range of flower colours, from white to scarlet; however, it was the pink fern that was chosen as the State's flower. The pink-flowered common heath is found only in the Grampian mountains in western Victoria.

Kangaroo-paws are found only in Western Australia. The brilliant red and green Mangles' kangaroo-paw is the floral symbol of the State. Kangaroo-paws are curious, lily-like plants with the flowers resembling outstretched fingers on the end of thin, long arms. The flowers are covered in small hairs giving them a velvet appearance. The flowers of Mangles' kangaroo-paw are collected for the fresh and dried flower market and many plants arc exported. Kangaroo-paws are only some of the hundreds of beautiful plant species which make up the world-famous springtime wildflower displays in the bushland around Perth.

The Sturt's desert pea is the emblem for South Australia and unlike the kangaroo-paw has no regular flowering season. Typical of many desert plants, it flowers in response to rain. The brilliant black-centred red flowers make a carpet of colour contrasting brilliantly with the sombre desert hues. After the plant flowers the hard seeds are shed and survive many years before conditions favour germination.

The Northern Territory's floral emblem, Sturt's desert rose, also celebrates one of Australia's most widely travelled inland explorers, Captain Charles Sturt. Sturt made observations of both the desert pea and desert rose, which now bear his name. The desert rose is a small desert shrub with dark green leaves. The flowers which often appear in late winter betray the desert rose's affinity with hibiscuses. The petals are mauve and the flowers have dark red centres.

The desert homes of the South Australian and Northern Territory emblems are a long way from the wet tropical home of Queensland's flower. The Cooktown orchid is, for an Australian orchid, very impressive. Up to twenty large white or mauve flowers are produced on a flower stalk and these make a fine indoor cut-flower display. They grow in the wild attached to tree trunks or exposed rock faces in wet forests of far northern Queensland.

The Cooktown orchid became Queensland's floral emblem as a result of a competition. In 1959 when the State was preparing to celebrate its centenary several plants were suggested as possible emblems. A Brisbane newspaper held a competition and over 10 000 entries were received. The Cooktown orchid was the clear winner with a grevillea as runner-up. It is a reflection of many Australians' perception of their native plants that third place in the competition went to a widely planted Mexican import, the poinsettia. In finally deciding on the floral emblem for the State the government wanted an easily cultivated native Queensland plant, which was decorative and distinctive in appearance as well as being maroon, Queensland's official colour.

The largest plant chosen as a State floral emblem is the Tasmanian blue gum. With a height of 70 metres and a trunk diameter of 2 metres it is hardly a plant to add to a flower bed!

The Tasmanian blue gum is a tree of the tall forests of south-eastern Tasmania and parts of Victoria. It is a valuable timber tree and is used for heavy construction such as poles, sleepers and piles. The tree is widely grown in New Zealand, South Africa, California and the Mediterranean region.

Unfortunately, the flowers are quite inaccessible and the tree is hardly suitable for a home gardener. The blue gum has not become as popular as a symbol as it might and this is probably due in part to its unfamiliarity to the average Tasmanian.

By contrast with the blue gum, the Australian Capital Territory has one of the smallest floral emblems. The delicate royal bluebell is a native of the high-country forests of the Australian Capital Territory, New South Wales and Victoria. The small violet-blue flowers are only 3 centimetres across but emerge in small clusters. This floral emblem is easily cultivated and grows from seed, cuttings or division of the roots. It is suitable for growing in small gardens or pots and this makes it accessible to many would-be gardeners.

Introduced plants

Australia's floral appearance has been altered for all time by the introduction of a wide variety of plant species from all over the world. Since no Australian plants provide any significant foods for Europeans all of the cultivated food plants are introduced. Many of the country's worst weed pests have come from seemingly innocuous exotic garden plants.

The most famous example of this is the prickly pear. It started originally as a curious pot-plant in a garden at Scone in the Hunter Valley in 1839. Within sixty years this aggressive weed had covered more than 4 million hectares of grazing country in southern Queensland. Hundreds of thousands of native birds were killed in an attempt to stop the spread of the seed. By 1925, some 25 million hectares of eastern Australia were covered with the pest and it was spreading at the rate of 100 hectares an hour. Those attempting to control the pest were lucky. An insect predator from the prickly pear's native homeland was introduced and the cactus disappeared almost overnight.

This remarkable result has not been achieved for other weed pests on anything like the same scale since. The best form of control is to keep potential new weed species from becoming established in the first place. Australia has very strict quarantine controls to protect the country's agricultural industries as well as the unique animals and plants.

The Gippsland waratah (Telopea oreades) *is the only type of waratah to grow into a tree.*◄

The most majestic of all Australia's wildflowers, the waratah is a striking plant when in flower. These shrubs and trees have tough, dark green leaves, often toothed, and the individual flowers grow on a dense head.

The waratah (Telopea speciosissima) *is the floral emblem of New South Wales. This plant grows to a height of 3 metres or more and can bear over fifty brilliant crimson flower-heads.*▼

Sturt's desert pea (Clianthus formosus) *is found throughout the drier areas of the continent.*

Drought is the typical mood of the arid scrublands but within a month of the violent heavy thunderstorms the wildflowers burst into life and the ground is a blaze of colour. (Page 137.)

The spectacular translucent red flowers of the Sturt desert pea are at their most striking when seen en masse.

Grevilleas—spider flowers—are among Australia's most attractive group of plants. Colourful and rich in nectar, the flowers have an irresistible attraction to birds. Grevillea confertifolia *(below) and (left)* Grevillea *'Poorinda Peter'.*

Hakea francisiana. *Hakeas vary from small shrubs to small trees with a wide range of leaf shapes.* ▲

The fragile Cooktown orchid (Dendrobium bigibbum), *one of the many beautiful wild orchids found in Australia.*◄

The floral emblem of Western Australia, the unusual red and green kangaroo-paw (Anigozanthos manglesii) *produces hairy tubular flowers at the end of a long, stiff stem.*

'Dwarf Delight', *a small variety of kangaroo-paw. Found only in Western Australia, there are eight kinds of kangaroo-paw, which resemble the Japanese iris in their growth.* ▼

Many Australian wildflowers have adapted to use birds rather than insects as pollinators. The large tubular flowers of the Christmas bell are shaped to ensure that the bird thrusts its head deep into the flower so pollen is deposited on its head.

The colourful bottlebrush is possibly the best known and most widely cultivated of Australian shrubs.

Bottlebrush flowers—crimson, yellow or greenish-white—are massed in dense cylindrical spikes and are carried like candles on the tips of the branches. ▼

Bottlebrush make a brilliant floral display. These hardy, bushy plants vary in size from 2 metre shrubs to small trees.

A study of perfection—the creamy yellow Banksia oblogifolia. *The banksia was named by the botanist Sir Joseph Banks who discovered it when he came to Australia with Captain James Cook.*

144

One of the most attractive of all banksias is the heath-leafed *variety*, Banksia ericifolia.

Banksia integrifolia, *a coastal shrub that colours the seascapes of Queensland, New South Wales and Victoria.*

Wattles are found all over Australia and rank so highly in the affection of the people that they have become the country's floral emblem. There are more than 500 varieties and the flowers range in colour from bright yellow through to deep orange. ▲

Massed pink flowers of the thryptomene, a member of the myrtle family, and the fluffy golden blooms of the acacia colour this outback scene. ►

Boxleaf wattle (Acacia buxifolia), a bushy yellow-flowered shrub growing in New South Wales. ◄

Few countries have such wealth of wildflowers as Australia. Parts of the continent are carpeted at various seasons with wildflowers of deep purple, vivid red, blue and green—orchids, boronias, pitcher plants, kangaroo-paws and countless species of everlasting flowers. ▲

Late afternoon hues of mauve and gold accentuate the graceful shape of these gum trees at Wyndham, Western Australia. ►

Waterlilies in Kakadu National Park, Northern Territory.▼

Mosses and ferns clothe the lower levels of temperate rainforest along the shores of Lake St Clair, Tasmania.

Spinifex grass, often called porcupine grass, is found on coastal sand-dunes and inland in warm areas with low rainfall. Spinifex clumps are the home of many geckos, skinks and insects. (Previous page.)

The solitary Cazneaux tree (known as this because it was made famous by Harold Cazneaux's photographs) stands sentinel on a grassy plain in the eastern part of the Flinders Ranges. Gum trees are a symbol of Australia's bushland and pastoral landscapes. ➤

The silvery, straight, smooth trunks of mature karri forest rise like columns from the undergrowth. The massive karri can grow to more than 60 metres.

North Queensland rainforest. Tree ferns, lush growth and dappled light filtering through the dense canopy are typical of rainforest in the tropical north. (Previous page.)

Scattered gums, boulders and rocky ridges make up the stark landscape on the Edgar Range in the Kimberleys, Western Australia. ▼

The gnarled trunk of a giant fig tree near Wingham in New South Wales.

A river meanders through luxuriant rainforest vegetation. Dense rainforest, ranging from tropical to temperate, is found in patches along the northern and eastern coasts of the continent and in Tasmania. ➤

Bangalow palms (Archontophoenix cunninghamiana) *adorn river banks in rainforest areas.*

The Australian baobab—the most grotesque tree in the continent. Sometimes called the bottle tree, its name is derived from the bizarre swelling of the trunk caused by internal storage of food and water against long periods of drought. (Left and previous page.)

From Australia's far north to the southernmost part of Tasmania, and from east to west, gum trees are present—wherever trees grow. ►

'Blackboys', or grass-trees, stand out like sentinels on the landscape. These thick-stemmed trees have a crown of long rigid leaves which grow in a dense tuft from which emerges a flower stem 2 metres long.

Snow gums are an excellent example of the adaptability of eucalypts. They survive above
the snow-line, almost overwhelmed by metres of snow during the winter, appearing in
fresh spring verdure when the first thaw comes. ▲

Small eucalypts, dazzlingly white barked, are scattered through the rocky spinifex country
and are commonly known as 'ghost gums'. (Page 168.)

The hardy mangrove, Fraser Island, Queensland. These trees have adapted to live in tidal
shallows where waterlogging and high salt concentrations would kill other trees.
(Following page.)

Gum trees typify the Australian landscape. There are more than 500 species of this hardy
evergreen which has adapted to all climatic conditions. ►

THE COASTAL
FRINGE

When one thinks of Australia's coastline, for many Australians it is not far away. Over 70 per cent of the population lives near the sea and even the country's largest inland city, Canberra, has less than 300 000 inhabitants. The Australian continent has a long and varied coastline shaped by seven different seas. For every Australian there is a favourite piece of coastline which may not be generally well known and is often associated with early childhood memories. The 38 000-kilometre-long edge of Australia has many stories to tell.

From the earliest times, maps and documents have referred to a country called *Terra Australis* and there has been speculation that Chinese navigators reached the shores of Australia well before the period of European discovery. It is well established that the so-called Macassans, from what is now modern-day Indonesia, reached the northern shores of Australia perhaps two hundred years before the first British settlement at Port Jackson.

In 1597, Wytflict's global map carried a rough representation of the eastern and western coasts of Australia which had apparently been charted by Portuguese navigators almost a hundred years earlier. Some years ago fishermen off Gabo Island netted a Spanish or Portuguese wine jar which tests at the Australian National University established as being about five hundred years old.

However, it was not until the seventeenth century, the so-called 'golden century of the Dutch', that navigators from that country charted most of the northern, western and southern coasts of the Great South Land. In 1606 they were in the Gulf of Carpentaria and in 1692 Tasman charted part of the coast of Tasmania before sailing on to New Zealand.

World-famous beaches

Australia is justifiably world famous for its beaches. Along the eastern coast the beach sand consists of pure quartz sand with very little broken shell or other material. At places where coastal cliffs are being rapidly eroded, beaches may be made of boulders or rock debris but these are the exception. Most of the sand that makes up the wide and beautiful beaches of Bondi, Manly and Surfers Paradise was first deposited there by wave action thousands of years ago.

Bondi is perhaps the country's best known surfing beach and is the closest ocean beach to the centre of Sydney. Bondi is a corruption of the Aboriginal name 'boondi' meaning 'the noise of the tumbling waters'. A land grant of 200 acres in 1809 effectively kept the now famous beach in private ownership until the 1870s.

Of course Bondi Beach is now very much a public place being visited by hundreds of thousands of people a year. During the summer, surf life saving events are held on this beach, maintaining a tradition that began in 1906. In the past the city beaches were the focus of many entertainments, not just swimming and sunbaking. The grand entertainment piers, beachfront bandstands and aquariums gave the beaches a festival aura. It is pleasing to see some of that festival magic slowly returning to the beaches.

Along many parts of the coast man has modified the foreshore by building seawalls and breakwaters or dredging channels for shipping. This often alters the pattern of wave action and sand removed from a nearby beach may not be returned. This is a serious problem for many local government authorities keen to maintain the appeal of their swimming beaches. A large portion of the annual budget of the City of the Gold Coast is spent on reclaiming eroding beaches. Many strategies are adopted to remedy the situation, ranging from construction of new structures to merely mining sand elsewhere and relandscaping the beach. The ocean is, however, relentless in its action and many 'solutions' are short-lived.

One natural beach formation which develops from a simple sand spit is a 'tombolo'. Tombolos are stretches of sand which connect one-time islands to the mainland. Two famous examples are the sandy isthmus at Sydney's Palm Beach connecting Barrenjoey with the mainland and the Yanakie isthmus connecting the granite massive of Wilsons Promontory to the main Victorian coast.

Last century the towering sandstone headlands guarding the entry to Sydney Harbour must have been a welcome sight for the thousands of new settlers who travelled to their new home. Having endured months at sea even those on 'forced passage' must have marvelled at the vast natural harbour they had entered. Typical of many similar harbours around the continent, Sydney Harbour is, to a geographer, a drowned river valley. This means that the harbour was once a deep river valley cut into the earth's surface which was flooded as the sea level rose. What we see now are the tops of the old hills and the sides of the valley dipping sharply into the sea.

Around the Great South Land

We will now set out on a journey of discovery of our own, circumnavigating the Great South Land, and we will start by heading north from Sydney to the beautiful waters of the Hawkesbury River estuary. This fine harbour is a drowned river valley which was first flooded about 17 000 years ago. Dotted with islands and hiding a myriad of tiny bays, this beautiful harbour gives us a glimpse as to the appearance of Sydney Harbour just two hundred years ago.

Aborigines would have been collecting oysters, mussels and pipis from the rock platforms. Perhaps a small wisp of smoke rose from a cooking fire near the water's edge. In the boulder-ridden slopes of the bays, Aboriginal men were hunting small wallabies, bandicoots and possums. Among the exposed mangrove roots on the edge of an incoming tide, the men and boys were hunting with spears the fish we now lure with rod and lines: bream, snapper, flathead, whiting and tailor.

The quiet beauty of these bays largely continues today. Where the land meets the water the mangrove forests create a rich feeding ground for fish and prawns. Over 60 per cent of commercial fish species are dependent on these waters. The nutrient-rich muddy shallows, thick with seagrasses, are the nursery areas for the growing fish.

The Hawkesbury's mouth, guarded by the Barrenjoey Headland, is wide and the tides are strong and it is unlikely ever to be locked off by sandbars. This has not been the case at Dee Why, Harbord and Narrabeen where coastal streams are blocked from entering the sea by sand-dunes. These dunes create the coastal lagoons which add beauty and character to Sydney's northern beach suburbs.

Our coast and islands tour now heads north above the sparkling lakes and rivers of the northern New South Wales coast. Across the border into southern Queensland we are now over Australia's beach and sunshine playground, the Gold Coast. A long stretch of beaches and lagoons, this coastal strip has seen some of the fastest urban development in Australia. Endless rows of high-rise buildings line the beaches and swamps and lagoons walled in for 'keys' developments. The main focus of the resort developments, the beaches have been eroding rapidly and much of the attraction of the beaches is diminished by afternoon shadows from the high-rise buildings near by. The rapid development of the Gold Coast, and the inadequacy of long-term planning, has lead to some major problems for residents and visitors alike. The Gold Coast and Surfers Paradise are places that seem to evoke either deep love or intense hatred.

The sand problems of the Gold Coast behind us, we continue up the coast to the sand mountains north of Brisbane. Just off the coast from Brisbane lies Moreton Island, a vast sand island rising 300 metres above the ocean. Mount Tempest, the highest point on Moreton Island, is the largest sand mountain in the world. Moreton Island is dotted with the shell remains of Aboriginal feasts and these are piled high in huge middens which are almost mountains themselves.

Sweeping northward past Noosa and the Noosa River we see one of the mainland's largest sand masses. Cooloola, now a national park, was once an island like Moreton and Fraser Islands to the south and north. The area is rich in sand formations such as perched lakes, extensive beaches and rainforest growing on pure sand. Cooloola's greatest claim to fame is its coloured sands, reached by tourist buses which drive along the beach.

Further north again is the greatest sand mass of them all, Fraser Island. The centre of a great conservation debate in the 1970s, Fraser Island was under threat from sand mining. The island is the largest sand island in the world and a rich source of the rare beach minerals rutile and zircon. In 1977 the Australian government banned the export of mineral sands from the island and it was added to the register of national estate. The island features a variety of distinct dune systems and lakes perched 100 metres above the sea on the dunes. Many habitats on the island are highly acidic and certain frogs and fish are uniquely adapted to these unusual conditions. These animals and the lakes themselves are of great scientific interest. The northern third of Fraser Island has been declared the Great Sandy National Park and a commercial forestry operation extracts timber from other parts of the island.

The Great Barrier Reef

Northward again and ahead lies one of the great wonders of the world, the Great Barrier Reef. Covering an area of 230 000 square kilometres or an area the size of England, Scotland and Wales, it is the world's largest coral reef province. It stretches over a coast length equivalent in North American terms to the distance between Washington and the Mexican border and has over 2000 individual reefs. The scale is difficult to comprehend since it is the largest structure built by living organisms.

Flying north over the seemingly endless reef we are unaware of how relatively recent this underwater wonder is. It is only in the last two million years that the Queensland waters have been warm enough to support such luxuriant growth.

As we pass over most of the famous resort islands like Hamilton, Great Keppel and Lizard, we realise there is a difference between them and the reef islands further out. Most of the resorts are built on islands which are solid rock and soil. They are continental islands or islands formed from pieces of the mainland stranded by rising seas. The true reef islands are sand cays surrounded by coral reefs. The only resort islands that are cays are Heron, Green and Lady Elliott Islands.

The Barrier Reef has one of the highest variety of living plants and animals in any given area of any habitat on the globe, including rainforests. From the tiny animals that build the coastal reefs to the turtles, dugongs and sharks that live in such profusion, the reef is a kaleidoscope of colour and movement.

As the reef slips by below us, it gets narrower and closer to the mainland. Off Cairns, the coral cay resort of Green Island is only 27 kilometres off the coast. Most of the reef is within 50 kilometres of Cairns. The reef continues to hug the coast most of the way up the eastern side of Cape York Peninsula and eventually pulls away and points northward to the coast of Papua New Guinea.

Marking the northern end of the Barrier Reef is Torres Strait. This dangerous passage is a graveyard of ships which was much used by merchantmen who had landed their cargo of convicts and stores in Sydney. Looking for a return cargo they headed north to the Dutch islands. Even in modern times, passage along the Great Barrier Reef and through the straits is a hazardous one.

Perhaps the most famous of all the Torres Strait wrecks is that of the *Pandora*. In 1790 the British Admiralty sent that little ship out to the South Seas to find the *Bounty* mutineers and return them to England for trial. Fourteen of those unfortunates were found in Tahiti but Captain Edwards did not know where Fletcher Christian and his eight companions were. So he dutifully set sail for England via Torres Strait with his captives confined in irons and placed in a cell on the quarterdeck. In Torres Strait, the *Pandora* went down with the loss of twenty-five lives but Edwards and the survivors, including ten of the *Bounty* mutineers, sailed to Timor in three small boats.

In Timor, by some strange fate, was a small group of convicts who had escaped from Sydney in a small boat. In that group was Mary Bryant and her husband with two infant children. The Dutch authorities handed them over to Edwards to be returned to England. The husband and the two children died on the voyage and only the redoubtable woman succeeded in getting home. She was eventually pardoned and the writer Boswell provided her with a small annuity. Six of the *Bounty* mutineers eventually went to the gallows.

Across the Top End

From Cape York west to the next major landfall we pass across the continent's only major indentation, the Gulf of Carpentaria. Over 650 kilometres across, it is a vast sea bounded on three sides by almost straight-sided, mangrove-lined coasts.

The vast Arnhem Land plateau marks the western boundary of this sea with its sandstone cliffs, vast seasonally flooded wetlands and termite-dotted hills. The string of islands that dot the coast of Arnhem Land, such as Wessel, Elcho and Croker, are now home to mission stations and Aboriginal settlements.

The largest of all these islands, and the largest Australian island (after Tasmania), is Melville Island lying between Darwin and the Arafura Sea. This largely flat island is over 100 kilometres long and is surrounded by huge swampy mangrove flats. The site of the first short-lived European settlement in northern Australia in 1824, the island has been the home of the Tiwi Aboriginal people for thousands of years. In 1978 the legal ownership of the island was given to the Tiwi Aboriginal Land Council. The council now runs all the affairs of the island including a major tourist attraction. After a short flight from Darwin, visitors can enjoy an insight to Aboriginal life and purchase traditional artefacts and the now famous Tiwi pottery.

The northern coast of Western Australia and the entire coastline of the Northern Territory show at many places the remains of the camps of Macassan fishermen who came looking for bêche-de-mer from about 1650. In 1803 as the great navigator Matthew Flinders sailed along the Arnhem Land coast he came upon six Macassan boats carrying 200 men and their leader told Flinders that there were a further 60 boats and over 1000 men along the coast.

Leaving the Top End and heading west and south we reach the broken northern coastline of Western Australia dissected with large, deep harbours. These are the drowned river valleys of the rugged Kimberley coast largely unknown to most Australians. Of the many large inlets, King Sound is the largest and it is almost landlocked. Over 100 kilometres long and about 50 kilometres wide, it is a large rectangular harbour protected from the sea by a string of inlets and reefs.

The western coast

Not only are the seas dangerous along this north-western coastline but the huge tides add to the risk. At Derby the rise and fall of the tide is over 10 metres.

Further south the character of the coast alters dramatically where the vast expanse of the central deserts reaches the sea. Viewing this scenic but arid coast centred on the Eighty Mile Beach, it is not hard to imagine why the early Dutch and Portuguese explorers and merchantmen had little enthusiasm when writing of their discoveries.

It was from one of these Dutch ships that Australia received its first white convicts almost 150 years before the first prison ships sailed into Botany Bay. The Dutch merchantman *Batavia* under Captain Pelsart ran aground on Houtman Abrolhos Island near the site of present-day Geraldton in 1629 and 250 terrified people managed to scramble ashore. Pelsart left the survivors and sailed to Batavia in a small boat for help. When he returned he found that there had been a mutiny in which over a hundred people had been murdered. Pelsart rounded up the mutineers and after conducting a very summary trial he executed most of the offenders but sentenced two to the unhappy fate of being marooned on the inhospitable Australian mainland near the mouth of the Murchison River. Wouter Loos and Jan Pelgrom were the first white men sentenced for murder in Australia. Their subsequent fate is unknown.

Further south, from Shark Bay to Western Australia's southern toe, is the 'limestone coast'. It is generally low, picturesque and very rugged. Wave action shapes the soft limestone into elaborate shapes including pedestals known locally as 'mushroom rocks'. One outcrop of limestone has been left by the encroaching ocean and is now a low island off Fremantle.

The natural beauty of Rottnest Island was observed by Willem de Vlamingh, a Dutch explorer, in 1696. Unfortunately, he gave the island a rather less than beautiful name, the Dutch equivalent to 'Ratnest'. How lucky we are that this name is now corrupted to Rottnest Island which has a rather quainter appeal.

In fact, the rats' nests that Willem noted were the homes of quokkas which are a species of small wallaby. The low, open nature of Rottnest Island means the quokkas are easily seen and they have become a feature of a visit to the island. Because of the ease with which quokkas can be studied in the wild and their suitability as a laboratory animal, they have been the most researched species of the kangaroo family. Much of what we know about the biology of kangaroos has come from studies of this little island-dweller.

Rottnest is a dry but naturally beautiful island which has developed as a tourist and holiday destination. Bicycles are the main means of transport. The island has had a variety of industries over the years, starting as a farming settlement and then variously a prison, a pilot station base, an internment camp, a World War II military base and most recently a viewing platform for America's Cup spectators.

Sea caves and arches typical of other limestone coasts add character and interest to this coastline which is in marked contrast to the ancient granites of Western Australia's southern coastline.

The grand national parks, like Fitzgerald River and Cape Arid of the granite-dominated southern coast, are noteworthy for their diverse landscapes. From Albany to the start of the Great Australian Bight the shoreline consists of spectacular granite cliffs, steep scree slopes and extensive beaches backed by dunes. The many small islands of the Recherche Archipelago are all part of the same granite landscape now isolated by the last rising of the sea.

The Great Australian Bight

The single most simultaneously dramatic and uniform feature of the whole continent's coastline is the Great Australian Bight. In a great arc over 200 kilometres long, the bight is the longest coastal formation of this type in the world. The dramatic effect is exaggerated by the fact that the Nullarbor Plain, treeless and flat, runs up to the edge of the bight without warning.

The vast, flat desert suddenly reaches the vast, flat ocean and all that joins them is a ragged cliff-line about 100 metres high. It is a dramatic contrast which draws the breath away. Once this was a sight which could be enjoyed by only a few intrepid adventurers but now, with a number of easy access points from the Eyre Highway, which links Perth with Adelaide, it is possible for motorists to take in the view. But be warned, the plethora of signs drawing attention to the dangerous overhanging edges of the cliff tops are warning of a very real danger.

On our journey of circumnavigation of the continent we now sweep down the mallee-covered Eyre Peninsula to the scattered islands that dot the entry to Spencers Gulf and St Vincents Gulf. The largest of these South Australian islands was named Kangaroo Island by Matthew Flinders.

Sculptured limestone cliffs, natural arches and massive granite boulders all provide contrast to the flat and rolling landscape that is Kangaroo Island (the continent's largest after Tasmania and Melville Island). The quiet north-facing bays and inlets are in contrast to the dramatic southern coastline which challenges the violent surges of the Southern Ocean. Here the wide, sweeping beaches are broken by headlands of older and sometimes curious rock formations. The most famous of these is Remarkable Rocks. This arresting natural work of art sits atop a granite dome which forms a tough and lonely headland pointing out to the sea. The strangely windswept boulders, some over 10 metres high, are clustered together as if in a forgotten sculpture garden. Admiral's Arch is a nearby natural rock archway which leads out to Cape Couedic.

Across the Backstairs Passage and on to the South Australian mainland our journey continues to the south. The long sand barriers of Younghusband Peninsula hold back the Southern Ocean from the lake systems of the mouth of the Murray River and the Coorong. As we pass the fertile southern corner of South Australia we swing to the east and follow the Victorian Great Ocean Road.

There are 'Twelve Apostles' that have made the western coast of Victoria famous. As for many other natural geological features, imaginative people have given highly anthropomorphic names to this collection of soft limestone sea stacks. The Apostles are joined by Lord Ard Gorge, named after a shipwreck, London Bridge and Thunder Cave. Weathered into strange shapes the Apostles are part of a beautiful and popular strip of coastline.

Where the long sweep of the western Victorian coast reaches the Cape Otway lighthouse we leave the mainland and cross one of the most treacherous stretches of Australian water, Bass Strait. Although only about 60 metres deep, the narrow straits concentrate the full fury of the violent westerly storms making the 200 kilometre crossing hazardous for small craft. Many parts of the coastline contain wrecks of the early settlement period of Australian history but not so many as Bass Strait. After it was established that Tasmania was in fact separated from the mainland the route from England to New South Wales was through Bass Strait. Many fine ships were lost in these wild waters. The strait is bounded on the east by the Furneaux group of islands and on the west by King Island.

King Island has the unhappy reputation as the marine graveyard of Bass Strait. It is now the site of Australia's main tungsten ore mines and a major refuge for seals. Flinders Island is the largest Bass Strait island and its name commemorates Matthew Flinders who first circumnavigated Tasmania and proved that it was indeed an island. The western side of the island is quite mountainous and much of the land is used for pastoral pursuits. In 1830 it was a reserve for the last of the Tasmanian Aborigines and it is now an important centre for Aboriginal communities.

Around Tasmania

The southern shore of Bass Strait is the indented coastline of Tasmania with its remarkable range of strange cliff and coast formations. From Tasman Peninsula, with its relics of the Port Arthur settlement, to Macquarie Harbour, this is one of the continent's most rugged coastlines.

Heading south down the Apple Isle's western coast we are soon off the coast of Australia's last great wilderness. This rugged and broken landscape drops to the ocean in a series of bays, rocky headlands and beaches. Hidden on this wind-lashed and largely uninhabited coastline are two harbours. The broad Macquarie Harbour has had its tranquil beauty broken by the conflicts between the hydroengineers and the conservationists. A great conservation battle has been won in protecting the vast south-western wilderness but the war will continue to be fought until most Australians appreciate the world significance of its protection and place the wilderness beyond compromise. Further south is the south-west's other great harbour, Port Davey.

Rounding South-West Cape and heading east again, we are soon over a group of small boulder-ridden islands known as the Maatsuykers. The main island is a dramatic pyramid-shaped peak reaching almost 300 metres and is topped with one of the country's most remote lighthouses. A dense wind-swept heath covering the island gives protection to many unique animals including the Tasmanian marsupial mouse.

East of the Maatsuykers and forming one side of the gateway into the Derwent River and Hobart is Bruny Island. A barren and windswept coastal island, Bruny has the reputation of being the first place apples were grown in the Apple Isle. The tree was planted by none other than the ill-fated Captain William Bligh.

The Tasman Peninsula, holding onto Tasmania by only a narrow spit of land, has a dramatic beauty. The towering dolerite cliffs of Cape Pillar rise 300 metres above the sea. The cape provides extensive views of Cape Raoul, Cape Hay and the lighthouse on Tasman Island. The cape is also the southernmost marker on that classic Australian ocean yacht race, the Sydney to Hobart.

Further north along the Tasman Peninsula the spectacular cliff formations include the Tasman Arch which has a roof 60 metres above the water level. This lofty arch is the remnant of what was once a sea cave. Near by, the Devil's Kitchen is a totally collapsed cave which is now a profound cleft in the rock containing a seething cauldron of surging water below. Not so violent but of great interest is the tessellated rock shore pavements at Eaglehawk Neck. These mudstones are so perfectly smooth and the weathering cracks in such perfect lines that they give the impression of human manufacture. In this rich area of coast there is a blowhole which concentrates the sea's fury and directs it into a spout of salt water and spray, apparently purely for the pleasure of tourists.

No account of the coasts and islands of Tasmania would be complete without reference to Macquarie Island and so before going back to Victoria we will head south into the great Southern Ocean. Macquarie is a tiny dot of land and life in the cold sub-Antarctic waters which is, by some administrative quirk, part of Tasmania. Discovered by sealers, as with all penguin and seal islands of the southern seas, the 5-kilometre-long island is 1300 kilometres south-east of Tasmania.

The coastal scenery is unlike anything on the mainland. First, there are no trees. As the mists roll down the steep hills the island has a distinctly Highland moors feel. The other overwhelming feature is the number of penguins. Everywhere you look the landscape is dotted or sometimes carpeted with penguins. Four species breed on the island and numbers of the royal penguin are estimated at 2 million birds. Their well-worn tracks from nests to ocean are so well used they look like paths in a formal garden.

Every year twenty or so Australians spend the winter on Macquarie and they are joined by others in the summer. Scientists, weather observers and support staff are conducting research into the natural phenomena of this sub-Antarctic island. The Buckles Bay base is located where Sir Douglas Mawson set up his scientific station on a narrow isthmus on the northern tip of the island in 1911.

The dramatic Victorian coast

We rejoin our circumnavigation of the Australian mainland on the western coast of Victoria on an island that is no longer an island. A bridge means that Phillip Island is no longer dependent on ferries to connect it to the mainland. Now only a ninety-minute drive south of Melbourne, it's a magnet for tourists.

A cold, windy beach on the western tip of Phillip Island is a strange place for a famous tourist attraction. All the more strange is that international visitors flock to the beach only at night. It is, of course, the evening parade of blue and white penguins which attracts the curious visitor. During the protracted breeding season these seafaring birds come to shore to either relieve duties at the nest or feed the young. The nests are in burrows among the sand-dunes. Since the penguins are wary of coming ashore, they wait in the water until a group forms and then come ashore in the safety of numbers. As a result, we now observe the famous 'Penguin Parade'.

Phillip Island boasts other wildlife-watching experiences including colonies of seals on rocks off the western end of the island and koalas which are widespread. Muttonbird or shearwater rookeries are also common on the coastal cliffs and dunes.

Gales are common in the waters of Bass Strait and in 1798, when caught in their open boat in rough seas, Matthew Flinders and George Bass found shelter on the lee side of a 'lofty hummocky promontory of hard granite'. This they subsequently named Wilsons Promontory. Bass and Flinders were followed south by sealers, timber-getters and pastoralists and the slowly disappearing evidence of their activities is still scattered along the lonely coves and headlands of this coast.

Wilsons Promontory is the most southern point of the Australian mainland. It is now a national park and is a popular bushwalking area. Long, dramatic trails along the boulder-stewn coastline find their way to secluded beaches. Always the lofty tops of Mount Ramsay and Mount Latrobe dominate the skyline.

We now journey along the softer seascapes of the Gippsland coast where the long sweeps of sand-dunes hold back kilometres of coastal lakes. Rounding Cape Howe, we are nearing the end of our travels as we head north along the New South Wales coast. Here, mountains are again close to the shore and rocky headlands and stretches of cliffs are common. The massive sandstone cliffs of Point Perpendicular face the sea at Jervis Bay and further north the Sydney sandstones create a spectacularly sculptured coast. The most notable cliffs are on the coast of Royal National Park which marks the southern boundary of metropolitan Sydney and nearly the end of our coastal explorations.

Now that we have circled the continent, there only remains to visit two far-flung islands of Australia. These Pacific Ocean islands linked by history and location have very different patterns of human settlement.

Lord Howe Island

Lord Howe Island is the only Australian island which has 'outstanding universal value'. As such it is one of Australia's six World Heritage areas and it is probably the country's best kept secret. Only 11 kilometres long and 2 kilometres wide, this tiny volcanic ocean speck is 700 kilometres into the Pacific from Sydney.

The sheer black basalt cliffs of Mount Gower rising to 875 metres, together with Mount Lidgbird, dominate the southern horizon of the island.

A low, flat area dotted with palms and native flowering plants connects the high mountains to a series of hills on the northern end of the island. As if this subtropical paradise was not already beautiful enough, a fringing reef and protected lagoon are the finishing touches to this idyllic land and seascape.

Lord Howe was given the honour of World Heritage status because of the pristine qualities of the natural environment and the interest and variety of plants, marine life and birds.

The banyan is one of Lord Howe's most unlikely trees. As the branches spread they drop new roots to the ground below. These aerial roots develop into new trunks and the tree keeps spreading. One 'tree' on the island is reported to cover 2 hectares of forest by this means. Lord Howe's palm trees are well known around the world as fine indoor plants. Although four species are known from the island the one most favoured for cultivation is the unique thatched palm, which was once called kentia palm.

Huge colonies of seabirds are a trademark of the Lord Howe Island group: providence petrels, muttonbirds and the large black and white masked booby. Perhaps the most attractive seabird is the aerobatic red-tailed tropicbird which when breeding has a flush of pink colour and a pair of long, red tail streamers. Many of the island's unique bushland birds disappeared in 1918 when rats arrived on the island, escaped from the grounded steamship *Makambo*. One Lord Howe bird species to survive, the woodhen, was the subject of a major conservation programme.

No visit to Lord Howe, even for the armchair traveller, is complete without a dive on the coral reef. It is the most southern coral reef in the world and is growing at the very coldest limits for coral growth. Although still delightful to the eye of the casual beachcomber, the number of coral varieties is much fewer than reefs growing in tropical waters. The coral is a great attraction to the snorkeller or glassbottom boat visitor but the fish are the main drawcard. Handfed for many years the fish are now very tame. The largest and most numerous species are the spangled emperor and the double-header wrasse. On the northern side of the island handfed fish include mullet, silver drummer and trevally.

Norfolk Island

Further out into the Pacific, another Australian island territory is famous not only for its beauty but for its contrasting history of human habitation.

Norfolk Island was the site of the second European settlement in the Australian region. About a month after Governor Phillip stepped ashore at Sydney Cove, Lieutenant King was dispatched to Norfolk Island to establish a settlement. Largely attracted by Captain Cook's description of the Norfolk Island pines and native flax and their suitability for use in shipbuilding and canvas making, Phillip decided to establish two penal settlements from the earliest days. Norfolk gained the reputation for being one of the harshest penal colonies where hardened criminals were sent for 'punishment short of death'.

After the convicts and their guards had left the tiny island in 1855 the vacant island was occupied by the descendants of the mutineers from the *Bounty*. Having survived for several generations on Pitcairn Island, west of Tahiti, the descendants were in need of a larger home. Norfolk Island was chosen and a British naval ship collected all of the Pitcairners and took them to their new home on Norfolk. Descendants of Fletcher Christian and his co-conspirators now live on Pitcairn and Norfolk Islands as well as Australia and New Zealand.

Norfolk Island is an undulating pine-tree-clad island with rich volcanic soils which is now becoming an important South Pacific tourist destination. The Norfolk Islanders now enjoy a level of political independence from Australia in many locally important fields. A great challenge facing the island is to balance the need for tourist development with the needs to preserve the qualities which make the island unique.

With a jet flight of a few hours we are back in Sydney and at the end of our circumnavigation of the island continent. In planes, boats and cars we have covered over 40 000 kilometres of some of the most spectacular coastlines on the face of the earth.

Darwin, capital of the Northern Territory which obtained self-government in July 1978. Darwin Harbour was discovered in 1839 by Lieutenant John Stokes in HMS Beagle and named after the naturalist Charles Darwin. (Previous page.)

Bathurst Island, home of the Tiwi Aborigines, north of Darwin. ◄

Chasm Island, an Aboriginal reserve off Groote Eylandt in the Gulf of Carpentaria. ▶

Showcase of the sea, the Great Barrier Reef draws visitors from all over the world. Many fascinating places are accessible by boat or plane and visitors can view the wealth of animal life—more per square kilometre than any other region on earth. ▼

Verdant coastline between Cairns and Port Douglas. Rich alluvial soil deposited by the state's many large rivers permits intensive agriculture on the coastal plain in northern Queensland.

Low Isles, north-east of Cairns, was the base for an historic British scientific expedition led by Sir Maurice Yonge in 1928–29 to collect corals from the Great Barrier Reef.

Sunset gilds Daydream Island, a popular resort in the Whitsunday Passage.

Lindeman Island, off Mackay, Queensland, is the oldest resort island off the coast and is a popular venue for family holidays.

Fraser Island, Queensland, the largest sand island in the world, is an example of the struggle between the wind which keeps the sand moving and the vegetation which tries to hold it. ➤

Bliss at the Hamilton Island Resort in the Whitsunday Passage, Queensland.

Surfers Paradise, Queensland, Australia's most popular holiday resort. ➤

Coolangatta Beach—one of the brightest stars among the stunning beaches that stretch for about 30 kilometres along the Gold Coast of Queensland. ◄

Sheltered bays with fine sandy beaches are a feature of Noosa National Park which encompasses the shoreline between Noosa and Sunshine Beach, Queensland. ▼

Ruins of the penal settlement at Trial Bay, near Kempsey, New South Wales. The gaol, opened in 1886, housed prisoners engaged in building a breakwater on the bay. Work on the breakwater was abandoned in 1903 and the gaol closed until World War I when it was used to house German internees.

The tip of the Barrenjoey Peninsula, Sydney—the beautiful surf-swept Palm Beach and the Pittwater, home of many millions of dollars' worth of luxury yachts. (Following page.)

Forster Beach, New South Wales.▼

Rough seas at the Gap, an extremely high cliff with sheer drops—unfortunately, the site of many suicides in east Sydney. ▲

Paradise for surf and sun seekers—Turimetta Beach with Narrabeen Beach in the background—two of Sydney's many sweeping northern beaches. ◀

Bondi Beach, Sydney, the best known surfing beach in Australia. The name is an abbreviation of the Aboriginal word 'boondi' which means 'the sound of tumbling waves'. ▼

189

The Moruya River flows into the ocean through the Moruya Heads on the southern coast of New South Wales. This river once provided access to the Araluen and Braidwood goldfields; now the surrounding area supports dairying, timber and oyster farming.

The spectacular blowhole at Kiama, New South Wales, sprays water to heights of 60 metres. (Previous page.)

Trawlers moored at Lakes Entrance, Victoria, home port for a very large fishing fleet.

Storm clouds bring a brooding dusk to Norman Beach, Wilsons Promontory, Victoria.
The promontory is the southernmost part of the Australian mainland.

Quaint, colourful and patriotic bathing sheds on the Mornington Peninsula, the boot-shaped promontory that provides Melburnians with a beachside playground.

Mariner's Lookout offers a panoramic view over Apollo Bay, an attractive tourist town on the Great Ocean Road, Victoria. ▲

Artistry of the sea—eroded rock formations at Port Campbell, Victoria. ➤

The Grotto, one of the many spectacular features of the highly sculptural seascape along the Port Campbell coast, Victoria. ▼

The sea thrashes and foams against the Hazards, a line of high granite hills on the mid-eastern coast of Tasmania.

Stanley and the Nut. The small Tasmanian crayfishing town of Stanley is dwarfed by the Nut, an impressive volcanic plug produced more than 10 million years ago.

Fishing boats at 'The Gulch', Bicheno. Crayfishing is the main local industry in this beautiful fishing port on the eastern coast of Tasmania.

Waves have produced a rare natural feature—the Tessellated Pavements—at the base of Eaglehawk Neck on the Tasman Peninsula, Tasmania. These plazas of rectangular paving blocks are caused by erosion along the joint lines of a very fine-grained sandstone.

Over the centuries the pounding seas and strong winds have created remarkable rock formations on Kangaroo Island, South Australia.

The mouth of the Murray River near Goolwa, South Australia.

Eroded coastal rock formations at Hallett Cove, near Adelaide.

A jetty stretches from Christies Beach to Port Noarlunga Reef in South Australia. The Port Stanvac oil refinery can be seen in the distance.

The unbroken wall of cliffs at the edge of the Nullarbor Plain on the Great Australian Bight stretches into the horizon. The incessant seas have undercut the limestone ramparts and brought down heaps of rocks at the base of the cliffs.

Cape Leeuwin—the most south-westerly point of Australia. The cape is named after the Dutch ship Leeuwin *which is thought to have sighted this part of the coast in 1622 while heading for Batavia.*

Twilight Cove, near Esperance on the southern coast of Western Australia.
(Following page.)

Shell Beach, a perfect sweeping expanse on the Shark Bay Peninsula, Western Australia.

Strikingly coloured weathered sandstone defines the coastline at Broome, Western Australia.

Water, salt and vegetation have combined to create these intricate tidal patterns in Cambridge Gulf, Western Australia. (Following page.)

Swimming and surfing are enjoyed at Scarborough, one of the beautiful Indian Ocean beaches near Perth.

OCEANS AND MARINE LIFE

The underwater world is one which most of us can only glimpse occasionally: photographs in a book, a documentary, a visit to an aquarium or perhaps the chance observation of a stranded animal on a beach. It is one of the last great frontiers for research and exploration.

The Australian continent is surrounded by some of the most beautiful and complex marine communities in the world, including the largest structure ever built by living creatures—the Great Barrier Reef. The marine world is one which can yield great economic benefit as is evidenced by the rich Australian oyster, prawn and fishing industries. It is also a place of great potential danger. Many inhabitants of the oceans are huge: the giant sperm whale, whale shark, manta ray and white shark. However, the majority are small, and arguably the smallest are the most important of all.

Coral polyps are a variety of tiny animals which form the framework for whole communities to live together in the shallow warm waters of the tropics. 'Coral reef' is the name we give to the whole reef system; corals, starfish, seaweed, crabs, shellfish, fish and turtles to name a few.

The hard corals have been called the 'architects' of the coral reef. Hard corals are formed by individual coral polyps which lay down a solid limestone base as they grow. The individual animals may be visible to the naked eye or may require a microscope to be seen. Each polyp is a separate animal but each is connected to form a colony. It is a remarkable situation of 'living together but separate'. As the polyps divide, a connection remains between each animal. The coral colony also has an entity of its own. Hard corals are a colony of living animals stretched as a veneer over a limestone base which they are constantly enlarging. Typical of the corals are the so-called brain corals and mushroom corals.

Soft corals do not have a solid limestone skeleton but have tiny chips of limestone in their bodies. The soft corals are not the reef builders in the sense that the hard corals are. Some soft coral colonies are mobile and others develop into large beautiful fans, fleshy forms like fungi or long strand whips. Perhaps the most dramatic are the lace-like forms of the gorgonian corals. Most are highly coloured, rich reds or yellows, a result of the coloured limestone chips embedded in their bodies. The colour of many corals, however, does not come from within. Most corals support millions of tiny single-celled plants which live within the tissues of the coral polyps. The coral benefits from the plant's ability to produce food from sunlight. These tiny plants also contribute to the living colour of many coral colonies, which explains why most corals lose their natural colours when the colony dies.

In contrast to the highly visible corals, much of the most important work in the sea is done by the myriads of usually invisible creatures that float in the surface waters of the oceans. These tiny plants and animals are collectively known as the plankton. The plants are usually single floating cells only made significant by the vast numbers of them. Tiny animals feed on the plants and larger animals then feed on them.

Moving along in this great melting pot of living forms are some larger well-known animals. These include the plankton-feeding giant whales, manta rays and the whale shark. Equally well known, but for quite different reasons, are the floating jellyfish which are themselves colonies of individual animals.

Fearsome jellyfish

Although fascinating in their own right, some species of jellyfish are known only because of the fear they evoke. The box jellyfish, or sea wasp, of the waters of

Queensland and the Northern Territory has caused the deaths of over seventy people in Australian waters since 1900. Summer is the most dangerous time but box jellyfish can move close inshore at any time of the year. They are predators and feed on prawns which they catch with their long tentacles and immobilise with their strong venom. On hot, calm, overcast days in summer, the box jellyfish is forced to feed closer inshore and this is when swimming is particularly dangerous. As a swimmer cuts across the trailing tentacles, the tentacles break off, injecting a strong venom. In children death can follow in minutes. Fortunately an antivenom has been developed and this is kept on hand in many surf life saving clubs. Other tropical jellyfish can cause painful stings but only one other is known to cause death.

In southern Australia the bluebottle jellyfish causes inconvenience and discomfort to swimmers. It has a gas-filled float which it uses to catch the wind and sail along on the water. Hanging from the float is the feeding tentacle which may be up to 10 metres long. Bluebottle tentacles can sting in the water and are also dangerous if picked up after being washed onto the beach. Bluebottles may congregate in large numbers and sometimes become a serious enough problem to close swimming beaches.

It is unfortunate that the most richly coloured and beautifully adorned sea inhabitants should have to suffer under the decidedy unattractive name of sea-slugs. Nudibranch is probably preferable but is only a slight improvement. The nudibranchs are shellfish which have abandoned their shells and gain protection from being highly visible but bad tasting.

The variety of lifestyles and special adaptations of the 2000 or so different Australian nudibranchs is probably matched only by their extraordinary range of colours and shapes.

Nudibranchs are like koalas in that they are most particular about their diet. Each species has very special needs. They are all carnivores. One common species feeds only on certain species of barnacles, another species solely on the eggs of other nudibranchs.

Nudibranchs are great thieves. One species, which feeds exclusively on bluebottles, carefully collects the poison cells of the jellyfish which are then placed together in a special organ of the nudibranch for its own protective use. Another nudibranch species has a similar arrangement with the deadly sea wasp or Queensland box jellyfish.

Giant clams

Giant clams have certainly not abandoned their shells and are the giants of the shellfish world. When mature, a large specimen can be over a metre across. The Great Barrier Reef is the home of the giant clams and all of the world's different types are found in its waters.

Giant clams are both male and female. On certain moonlit nights in summer a giant clam will come into breeding condition. For several hours the clam will shoot a stream of male sex cells into the reef water. The jet of water is enough to disturb the water surface a metre above. Once the sperm have been released the same clam then releases eggs into the water. If a large number of breeding clams are living close together the chances of fertilisation of the egg increase significantly.

The fertilised egg becomes a microscopic animal which swims freely for about a fortnight. It then settles into the sand and within two years is a small but easily recognisable giant clam.

Dried or frozen meat from giant clams fetches high prices on the markets of Hong Kong and Singapore. The entire body except the kidney is edible but the high-priced cut is the sweet muscle that opens and closes the giant clam's two shells. On the Great Barrier Reef in the last few decades many foreign fishing boats, mainly Taiwanese, have been illegally poaching giant clams. It has been estimated that the clam meat on vessels apprehended in the last dozen or so years had come from half a million clams. This over-harvesting of giant clams is having a major impact on the clam population of the reef.

Research is now in progress on the Great Barrier Reef and elsewhere in the Pacific to see whether the commercial market can be supplied with giant clams from ocean farms, perhaps like the oyster farms around Sydney. These could also be used to restock reef areas depleted through over-harvesting.

Cone shells are a small but colourful shellfish family. Popular with shell collectors because of the attractive shells, the cones are lethal hunters. Usually feeding on marine worms, snails or sometimes fish the cones are equipped with hollow-tipped poison 'harpoons' with which to poison prey. The toxins are fast acting and highly venomous. The species which poison fish have toxins capable of killing a fully grown human. If it is necessary to handle a living cone a sharp eye must be kept on the long flexible proboscis which protudes from the narrow end of the shell.

A distinctive and common group of shellfish typical of all Australian rocky shorelines are the chitons. Like little sea-going armadillos, the chitons have a shell made up of eight separate plates. They shun the daylight and cluster together under large boulders as the tide recedes. If disturbed a chiton will glide away across the surface of the rock to find a safer hiding location. The chiton is as firmly attached to the rock surface as any of its other shellfish relations.

Shellfish which are not committed to a relatively sedentary lifestyle are the squid and octopus. Fortunately our coastlines do not support populations of the 20-metre-long giant squid of the ocean depths that are the food of the sperm whale, but coastal squid and octopus have their own interest and danger.

Octopuses are as at home in open water as in a rock pool. They are proficient swimmers using an original form of jet propulsion to move about. On the seashore octopuses get about by 'walking' using their eight tentacles or arms. The suckers on their arms are used in catching their prey as well as moving about.

The blue-ringed octopus is a brilliantly coloured but dangerous small octopus found in all coastal waters. It is dark brown in colour with fleckings and circles of blue over the body and arms. When the octopus is taken from the water the circles become a brilliant blue, which is the octopus's warning. Normally the poisonous saliva is sprayed over a crab which after a few minutes is paralysed, allowing the octopus to capture its victim. If handled out of the water, the octopus injects the poison using its strong biting mouth parts. The effect of the toxin to a human is to cause paralysis, and death occurs through loss of breathing. The best first aid is artificial respiration.

With apologies to Paul Hogan, Australia has no edible shrimps. Nor do we have any lobsters. But we do have fine edible crustaceans. To give them their correct names, all of Australia's edible 'shrimps' are really prawns. And no North Atlantic lobsters have ever been harvested in Australian waters but then our range of edible marine crayfish are more succulent anyway! Other members of this group of marine animals which often grace the tables of fine restaurants and suburban homes alike are the various large mud and swimmer crabs and the deepwater Balmain (or Moreton Bay!) bug. The smaller rock crabs are often used for bait by fishermen and of course provide endless beachtime entertainment for small children.

However, our interest in crabs need not be focused totally on our own culinary or other satisfaction. Crabs perform some remarkable migrations which probably need to be seen to really be believed. For example, on far-flung Christmas Island, a piece of Australia closer to Singapore than the Australian continent, red land crabs rule the island during their annual migration. On an island little more than 20 kilometres across, 100 million land crabs are on the move in summer headed for the ocean to lay their eggs. The fact that a million crabs are accidentally killed every year on the island's roads is 'not significant for the crab's survival as a species'! When the crabs are on the move on Christmas Island everyone keeps doors closed to stop the houses being overrun.

Our controversial starfish

Starfish do not usually cause controversy but one Australian starfish certainly has. There are hundreds of species and they range from the small round-shaped starfish of the beach rock pools to the brilliant blue sea star of the northern coral reefs.

Although starfish feed in a variety of ways, some have developed a method of feeding outside of their bodies. The starfish wraps itself around the stationary prey and by spreading its stomach over the victim dissolves its fleshy parts with digestive juices. Having fed, the starfish withdraws its stomach and moves on, leaving behind the bleached skeleton of its prey.

This is the feeding method of Australia's most infamous starfish, the crown-of-thorns. This starfish may have up to twenty-three arms although about sixteen is usual. The arms are covered in long, very sharp spines. The prey species of this attractive starfish are the tiny coral polyps, the animals that build the coral reefs.

In low numbers, the crown-of-thorns is hardly noticed on a reef. It feeds at night and hides during the day. However, in parts of the Great Barrier Reef the crown-of-thorns is now in plague numbers. Aggregations occur on about 10 per cent of all the reefs that make up the Great Barrier Reef. Reefs that are badly infested with crown-of-thorns have large areas of dead coral which may take up to forty years to regrow. Scientists are at odds as to whether this is a major problem for the reef or simply a normal cycle in the balance of coral growth and decay.

The most widespread scientific opinion concerning the crown-of- thorns threat is that it is a natural occurrence and not compounded by activities of man. It is felt that during floods along the Queensland coast, higher than normal levels of nutrients are washed into reef waters. These nutrients produce more algae growth, meaning that more immature starfish larvae survive. Since one female starfish can produce over a million eggs and very few survive to become starfish, a relatively minor increase in survival of starfish youngsters can provide large increases in future populations. The earliest crown-of-thorns outbreaks on the Great Barrier Reef in the early 1960s are attributed to the 1959 Queensland cyclones.

A few scientists are not so convinced and believe that the crown-of-thorns threat is being underestimated. We are still a long way from knowing the real truth about this prickly starfish and much research is continuing into the phenomenon.

Australia's first export industry was based on the collection and processing of a relative of the starfish. For hundreds of years before the settlement of Sydney, the northern Australian coastlines were visited by Indonesian traders. They are collectively known as the Macassans since most came from that port in southern Sulawesi. They made their journey to collect trepang, or bêche-de-mer. These worm-like animals are common in the shallow tropical waters of northern Australia. Several different species were harvested but all are large, relatively inactive, sausage-shaped animals which filter the sand in search of food. The Macassans traded the processed trepang with the Chinese who use it in soups, with vegetables or fried. It is sad but this industry died about the same time that government regulations were brought into force to 'control' the industry and to collect duties.

Scientists are baffled as to how so many fish species can live together in small patches of ocean floor or reef. Coral reefs have the highest density of backboned animals in any habitat, marine or terrestrial. Surely competition should eventually reduce the numbers of species? It seems not.

There is huge variety in the shapes, colours, lifestyles and sizes adopted by this familiar group of animals. There are the huge reef cods which become so tame they can be approached by divers. Then there are fish that change sex if need be and the clown anemone fish which finds refuge among the stinging tentacles of anemones. The beautiful array of the dozens of species of angelfish and butterfly fish is a kaleidoscope of patterns and colours. There are fish like the stonefish which can kill you if you tread barefooted on their spines and there are the dozens of edible fish which are displayed in the city fish markets. Of all the fish, those which demand our interest and fear are the sharks, the great predators of the sea.

Sharks and rays

The sharks and rays are the most primitive of all fish and have changed little over the last 200 million years. These fish have no 'bones' but their bodies are supported by a tough, flexible cartilage. Over 140 species of sharks and rays have been recorded in Australian waters.

The largest of all the sharks is also the most harmless. Whale sharks are found in tropical waters, grow up to 18 metres and can weigh over 15 tonnes. Fortunately this giant feeds on microscopic sealife and is not a danger to divers. This is certainly not the case with many other large Australian sharks which will attack man for no apparent reason.

The most feared of these sharks is the white shark, or white pointer, of *Jaws* fame. Found around the world, this highly feared shark grows to over 7 metres in length. The largest specimen caught on a line was taken at Ceduna in South Australia. This massive shark measured over 5 metres in length and weighed over a tonne. Despite the size and ferocity of this shark, the human victim is often not eaten and a few people have survived attacks. This shark can be found in inshore waters in any part of Australia.

Tiger sharks get their name from the stripes that are distinctive of younger animals. Adults grow to 6 metres in length and are one of the most feared predator animals in tropical waters. They are sluggish sharks feeding on a variety of fish, turtles, stringrays and shellfish. They are known to eat rubbish such as packing crates and in the 1930s a recently captured aquarium fish spat out an undigested tattooed human arm. This developed into the notorious 'Shark Arm' case which led to a murder being discovered, followed by a successful prosecution. During the murder trial it was revealed that the arm had been removed from the victim's body prior to the shark eating it.

Other known man-eating sharks include the mako, which is the most popular shark gamefish, the blue shark and a number of species of whaler sharks.

The grey nurse is a shark of the shallow offshore reefs of southern Australia. This shark may have been incorrectly held responsible for many attacks on people in the past. Despite its 4 metre length and savage-looking teeth it doesn't worry divers and is quite at home in large aquariums. This shark is becoming quite rare through hunting pressure and many conservationists are advocating its complete protection.

Despite the fear we have of sharks, divers have come to understand the behaviour of some of the larger sharks and know which ones to avoid. For example, the white-tipped reef shark, which grows to over 2 metres, is well equipped to attack divers but has the reputation of being 'fairly placid'. This is not necessarily the case with the similar-sized grey reef shark which sometimes gathers in schools of twenty or thirty! In these circumstances it is recommended that divers leave the water!

The possibility of a shark attack evokes a deep fear in most people. The idea of being eaten by another animal brings on a level of fear quite out of proportion to its possible occurrence. The fact is that Australians are more likely to be killed in a car accident while driving to the beach or to drown than to be taken by a shark. There is more chance of being hit by lightning than shark attack.

Until World War II, Australia had the notorious reputation of having the highest incidence of shark attack in the world. In the late 1930s a programme of shark netting was introduced on the most popular beaches in Sydney and Newcastle. In the twenty years prior to netting, over forty people were taken from the ocean and harbour beaches in these cities. In the forty years since netting began, only nine people have been taken. Of these, seven were taken in Sydney Harbour which has never been netted.

The success of netting sharks has lead to a false belief that these beaches are safe from shark attack. This is certainly not the case. A shark-netted beach doesn't have a solid mesh wall around it, excluding all sharks. Fish contractors place nylon gill nets 500 metres offshore on a certain number of days a year. The nets do not enclose a beach. The effect is that a certain number of sharks are caught every year around the major swimming beaches. How has this so dramatically reduced the incidence of shark attack? The probable answer is that although there are still large numbers of sharks, the reduction in shark numbers means that more natural food is available to the remainder. These sharks are not then pressed into taking food (that is, people) from shallow waters, like beaches. The very slight chance of being taken by a shark is therefore reduced even further.

Despite the observed success of shark netting in reducing human fatalities, the netting programme is not without its critics. They point to the high costs of the programmes and the large number of rare and harmless species accidentally killed. In Queensland since 1962, 468 rare dugongs, over 2500 turtles, 317 dolphins and two whales have been caught. This is not to mention the unknown ecological effects of a permanently modified shark population on the marine ecosystem near our beaches. It is a biological problem which is very difficult for accurate scientific study.

A number of curious small sharks are found in Australian waters and these include the Port Jackson shark. These flat-headed harmless little sharks live on sea-urchins, crabs and shellfish. Although various species of Port Jackson shark occur around the world they were first discovered at Port Jackson in 1788, hence their local name.

Just as curious but by no means harmless is the group of sharks called wobbegongs. They are flat, beautifully patterned sharks growing to about 2 metres which can cause nasty maulings. This is a shark which relies on camouflage and when its prey, usually a crab or octopus, comes near, it lunges forward to grab it. Attacks usually happen only when divers provoke or spear the shark.

The 'birds' of the oceans

Similar to sharks in having no bones, the rays are the 'birds' of the oceans. Even the smaller stringrays have a wonderful avian quality as they float through their liquid sky. But the manta rays are really the kings of the watery skies. With 'wingspans' of over 4 metres the manta rays flow slowly through the water like huge eagles. However, manta rays are not predators in the usual sense. Their cavernous mouths are opened as they pass through shoals of microscopic ocean life or tiny fish. Like the blue whale, and the whale shark, they sieve their food items from the water.

A manta ray's unusual appearance is matched only by its unusual behaviour. The most well known of these is the famous manta ray leap. The sight of a huge manta ray leaping from the water and falling back with a resounding crash, and repeating the display several times, must be quite awe inspiring. One would also expect it to be rather alarming if the observations were made from near by in a small boat! The reason for these displays is unknown. It has been suggested that the ray is trying to dislodge annoying parasitic fish from its mouth or fins.

Divers, especially those on fixed oxygen lines from boats, are nervous of manta rays. One unfortunate diver in waters off Thursday Island, near the northern tip of Queensland, was killed when his oxygen was cut off by a large ray. Although usually harmless, mantas are often known as devil rays. It is perhaps fortunate that these huge tropical fish do not possess the stinging barbed tail of their smaller relatives.

A large number of stingray and skate species live in Australian waters. They are easy to distinguish by their long, whiplike tail and wide, flat bodies. Stingrays spend most of the time buried in the sand where they feed on shellfish, crabs and sea worms. When disturbed in shallow water by a swimmer, they break free of their sandy hiding spot with vigorous flapping of their 'wings'. Having located a stingray it is not wise to approach too closely since they have sharp spines on the tail. These spines are filled with venom. The ray will strike rapidly with its tail and, as well as being intensely painful, the venom can cause death. Since large rays often feed at night in shallow water it is wise to wade in the dark with great caution.

Marine animals which do not require careful approach are the ocean-living turtles. They immediately appeal to our sense of wonder and amazement. A large sleepy-eyed female turtle patiently drags herself up from the sea to lay her eggs. Hours later she goes back to the sea, not to return to land until the next breeding season. It is like having a visitor from another age or another world. The tiny youngsters follow her to the water a few months later, not to return for perhaps fifty years. How such vulnerable animals survive the rigors of ocean life, where they live, how long they live, we don't know.

Six species of marine turtles occur in tropic Australian waters. Five of these nest regularly on the Australian mainland and island beaches. The most common are the green and loggerhead turtles which breed throughout the tropical waters. Raine Island is typical and is one of the two largest turtle rookeries in the world. A flat, treeless sand speck off Cape York in far northern Queensland, it is a mecca for turtle researchers. Each summer the female green turtles congregate in the waters surrounding the islet. Every few weeks each female comes laboriously ashore to dig a nest hole and deposit her eggs. So many green turtles nest there that, late in the summer, eager females are digging up previous nests in an attempt to lay their eggs.

Our rarest marine turtle

The rarest marine turtle to nest on Australian shores is the curious leathery turtle. This turtle is unlike other marine turtles since it has no hard shell. Fortunately for the leathery turtle, this means that it is not part of the trade in turtle shells and this gives it some protection from human predators. However, in many other parts of the world the eggs of this turtle are collected for human consumption. It is hoped that the beaches around Bundaberg will continue to attract leathery turtles to nest in Australia. There is a major opportunity for protection of these remarkable reptiles at the same time as developing a major attraction for summer visitors to central Queensland.

The marine mammals of Australian waters have not fared well under the heavy hand of hunting by man. All of the seal species have declined dramatically in the last two hundred years and one species, the elephant seal, no longer breeds in continental

Australian waters. Australia probably has the largest population of dugongs remaining in the world but this is threatened by a variety of pressures. Of the thirty-six species of whales and dolphins recorded in Australian waters only the dolphins have not been under hunting pressure. In fact, north of Perth one species of dolphin is given free handouts of fish in a local custom which is rapidly becoming a tourist attraction.

Whales and whalers

The two most important whales for the nineteenth-century whalers were the southern right whale and the sperm whale. The right whale, so named because it was the 'right' whale to catch, has large baleen plates with which to sieve tiny animals from the water. The right whale was hunted for its oil as well as the large baleen plates which were used to make corsets. The sperm whale has teeth since it lives on squid which it may catch at a depth of over a kilometre below the water surface. It was hunted for its oil and a valuable wax which is concentrated in its large head.

The whalers of the early nineteenth century usually worked from ships, not a land-based station, and followed the whales. In the summer months they hunted sperm whales in the tropical waters. In the winter, as the southern right whales headed north from the sub-Antarctic waters to breed, the whalers were waiting. Right whales had major winter breeding areas off the southern coasts of Australia. Right whales were hunted along the southern coast of Western Australia, in South Australian waters, around the coast of Tasmania and off southern New South Wales.

Right whales are distinctive in being large whales with a smooth, finless back. They average 15 metres in length but a large animal can reach 18 metres and 100 tonnes in weight. Once widespread in both the Northern and Southern Hemispheres the total world population has not recovered from the nineteenth-century hunting. The world population is put as low as 2000 individuals.

Fortunately, in coastal southern Australia a small number of female whales are now returning to breed in the shallow inshore areas. Right whales are increasingly likely to be seen off Australia's southern coasts during the winter months. Near Warrnambool in western Victoria breeding females and their calves are present within a few hundred metres of the beach from May to September. Viewing platforms have been built and Warrnambool is now experiencing a well-appreciated winter tourism boom.

When the right whale population crashed through over-hunting, attention was turned to humpback whales. Like the right whales, humpbacks are baleen whales which feed in the cold sub-Antarctic waters in summer. In the winter months they head north along recognised migration paths, to breed in warm waters. The main Australian wintering grounds are in the Coral Sea and off the north-western coast of Western Australia. Humpbacks can reach 17 metres in length and weigh up to 50 tonnes. The diagnostic feature of this whale at sea is the tiny fin and arched back of the surface-swimming animal. This is the most likely large whale to be seen along the Australian eastern or western coasts. From June to August they are heading north to breeding grounds and from September to November heading south, back to the cold sub-Antarctic waters where their main feeding grounds are found. Humpbacks can breed only every second year since the 1.5 tonne calf is born after a twelve months' gestation period and remains with its mother for another year.

The tide turned against the humpbacks early this century when whalers began harvesting the large concentrations of animals in the cold southern waters. With the coming of the large floating factory ships this harvest became even more thorough. Land-based whaling stations in Australia at Moreton Bay, Byron Bay, Eden, Norfolk Island and Albany continued to harvest humpback whales, some until 1962. The worldwide population of these whales had collapsed from several hundred thousand animals to about 5000. Humpbacks were given worldwide protection in 1963. About 10 000 humpbacks used the Australian east coast migration route in 1949 and by 1962 this was reduced to about 300. Humpback whale populations are now starting to show some increase and it is possible for a new generation of Australians to easily see whales in the wild.

One of the most curious aspects of whale behaviour is stranding. Every year, some whales, somewhere on the Australian coast, launch themselves on the beach in what appears to be senseless self-destruction. Sometimes these strandings occur in large numbers. Why do whales do this? This question was first asked in the third century before Christ by the Greek philosopher and naturalist Aristotle:

It is not known for what reason they [dolphins] run themselves on dry land.

Over 2000 years later we are almost no closer in coming to an answer. Some suggest that it is suicide, since in massed strandings rescued animals persist in returning to the beach to join their dying companions. Others claim that whales are attempting to travel over ancient migratory routes that are now blocked by land and sandbars. It is possible that sick or injured members of the herd may deliberately strand and their distress draws in the rest of the highly sociable group. The clearest explanation to date is that irrespective of the reason for the first individual stranding (sickness, disorientation, parasite infection, panic in shallow waters, etc.) in social herds the remainder of the herd then follows to be with the animal in distress. To attempt to get a clearer understanding detailed studies of strandings are looking at a wide range of factors such as unusual tides, shape of the coast and the sea bottom, age, health and sex of animals stranding, and weather conditions at the time.

Seals, sea lions and mermaids

Almost as clumsy on land as a stranded whale, seals are now making a comeback after heavy exploitation over two centuries. The major concentrations of Australian seals are in Bass Strait, the coastal islands of South Australia and the south-western coast of Western Australia. Of the true seals only the southern elephant seal ever breeds in mainland Australian waters. There are colonies on King Island in Bass Strait, on Macquarie Island and on other sub-Antarctic islands. The massive male elephant seals weigh up to half a tonne and are immediately recognisable by their huge proboscis.

Three species of eared seals breed in colonies on Australian islands. The Australian fur seal is the largest of our resident seals. The males are distinguished by a large mane of coarse hair. The colonies of this seal are restricted to islands centred on Bass Strait. Despite huge hunting pressures up to the turn of this century, Australian fur seals now number about 20 000.

More widespread are the New Zealand fur seal and the Australian sea lion. Both these species occur in South Australian waters and off the coast of south-western Australia. The Australian sea lion is the only member of the seal family unique to Australia. Both these species can be seen on Kangaroo Island off the South Australian coast. Over 500 fur seals breed at Cape du Couedic, and 50 kilometres along the coast at Seal Bay about the same number of sea lions breed. At Seal Bay there are always some seals present since they do not appear to have a regular annual reproductive cycle. Kangaroo Island was an important base for seal hunters from Hobart and Sydney prior to the settlement of Adelaide. Not only could seals be procured for their skins and blubber but the arid climate of the island produced an abundant supply of salt for curing the skins.

Dugongs are not seals or dolphins but are distantly related to both. Dugongs are sometimes known as sea-cows, which is not a bad analogy. They are the only marine mammal that feeds totally on seagrasses. Dugongs are slow-swimming, 2-metre-long mammals found in tropical waters throughout the world. Despite the tiny eyes they appear to have good sight and certainly have excellent hearing. When not subject to hunting pressure they form in herds of a hundred or more.

Dugongs are certainly not graceful creatures but they have a contented and somehow friendly look. Nevertheless, it is hard to imagine the wild thoughts of fantasy of the homesick sailors who saw visions of mermaids when dugongs swam by.

Australia is one of few places in the world where dugongs are still relatively common. The main natural predators of an adult dugong are killer whales, large sharks and estuarine crocodiles. This declining species is now, sadly, under threat from accidental capture in fishing nets, poaching and possibly illegal hunting by Aboriginal hunters using non-traditional methods.

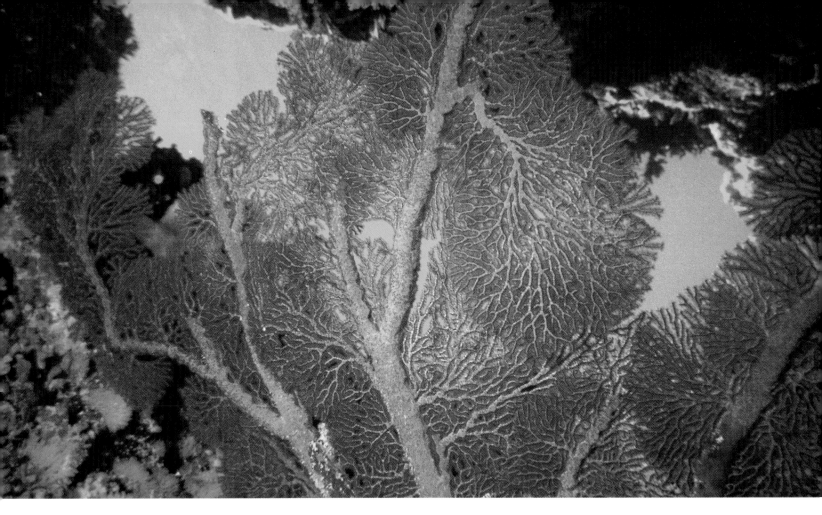

A brilliant clump of gorgonia coral on Marion Reef off Mackay, Queensland.

The Great Barrier Reef, which stretches some 2000 kilometres along the Queensland coast, is the most remarkable coral reef system in the world. (Previous page.)

Tubastrea coral polyps feeding. Voracious feeders, they use their tentacles to harpoon copious quantities of microscopic organisms such as zooplankton.

In the 1960s the Great Barrier Reef suffered a 'plague' of coral-feeding crown-of-thorns starfish (Acanthaster planci) which was thought to be threatening the very existence of the reef. Today, the acanthaster populations appear to be back to more normal levels.

Michaelmas Cay, Queensland. Cays consist of sand and broken coral that has built up, usually on the protected leeward side of the reefs. They are normally vegetated by plants which have been carried there as seeds by the wind, sea or birds. (Page 217.)

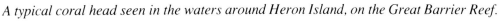

A typical coral head seen in the waters around Heron Island, on the Great Barrier Reef.

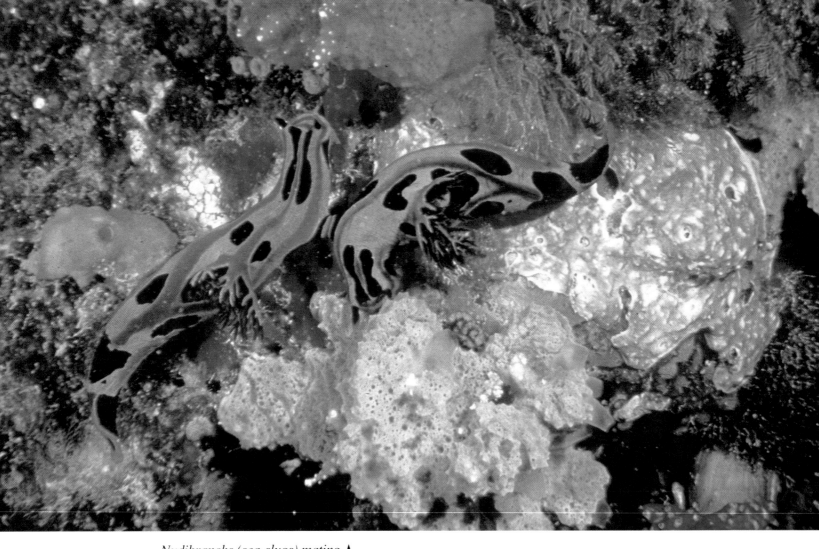

Nudibranchs (sea-slugs) mating. ▲

A colourful sea-slug, or nudibranch, drifting in shallow waters at night. These marine molluscs are related to snails and have no shells, quills or mantle cavities. ◄

The egg girdle of a nudibranch. ▼

Cucumaria frondosa, *a holothurian, or sea-cucumber, feeding at night. The feathery tentacles trap minute organisms in the seawater, the mouth opens and the whole branch is inserted into the opening. Between sixty and seventy species of holothurian have been recorded from Barrier Reef waters.*

A flamboyant tubeworm seen at Heron Island. The beautifully coloured reef species of marine worms are found in coral pools, under boulders or among coral rubble.

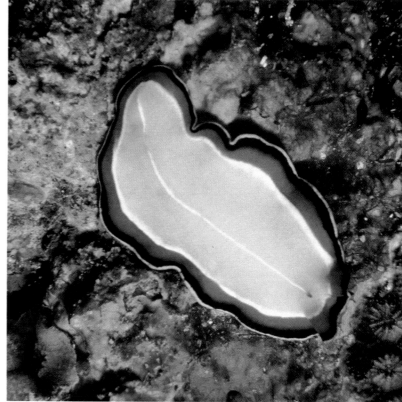

The leaf-like marine flatworm (Pseudoceros corallophilus). ▲

The seahorse, found in tropical and temperate waters around Australia. It swims in an upright position and has an outer bony skeleton of plate-like rings, a mouth at the end of a long snout and a curled tail which it uses to cling to seaweed. ◄

A brilliantly patterned coral crab, one of the many species of crustaceans found on the Barrier Reef. ▼

The most comical of reef characters—the hermit crab, seen here on Marion Reef. They have an unprotected abdomen and use the dead shells of molluscs for protection. When house-hunting, the small crab tests each shell it finds for size—an amusing sight for the observer.

Sponges are among the more conspicuous organisms to be seen on the Great Barrier Reef. This vividly coloured one was found at a depth of 20 metres on Wistari Reef in the Capricorn Group.

A needle-spined sea-urchin with characteristic five-fold symmetry — one of the most widely distributed sea-urchins on the coral reefs.

The strikingly marked coral cod (Cephalopholis miniatus) *rivals the coral trout in looks and flavour. In certain areas the wild populations of this species are being whittled away by . overfishing.*▼

The pufferfish, a common sight on the Barrier Reef where it is often found grazing on large massive corals. This strange little fish protects itself by expanding to twice its real size. ➤

Some 150 species of echinoderm (starfish, sea-urchins, etc.) add colour and interest to the Barrier Reef waters. Possessing amazing powers of regeneration, most starfish are able to replace lost or damaged arms.

The colourful little clownfish (Amphiprion noppopeus) *is one of several species that shelter among the tentacles of large tropical sea anemones.*

The elaborate Pterois antennata, *one of the many colourful inhabitants of coral reefs.*

One of the finest edible fish of the Barrier Reef, the coral trout (Plectropoma maculatum).

Bizarre and grotesque, the stonefish looks like a stone and lies camouflaged among coral on the Barrier Reef. It is the most venomous fish known and can kill anyone unlucky enough to tread on it barefooted.◄

The large, sluggish sea-cow (Dugong dugon) can be found in coastal waters and estuaries in Australia where they feed on vascular plants similar to eelgrass. ►

The cleaner wrasse (Labroides sp.) is one of the more unusual fish to inhabit tropical coral reefs. Seen here, this tiny fish is feeding off parasites infesting the mouth of a sweetlip.

Very common in shallow lagoons on the Great Barrier Reef, the tiger cowry shell lives in caves and ledges under reef ramparts, and is often found on top of micro atolls at low tide.

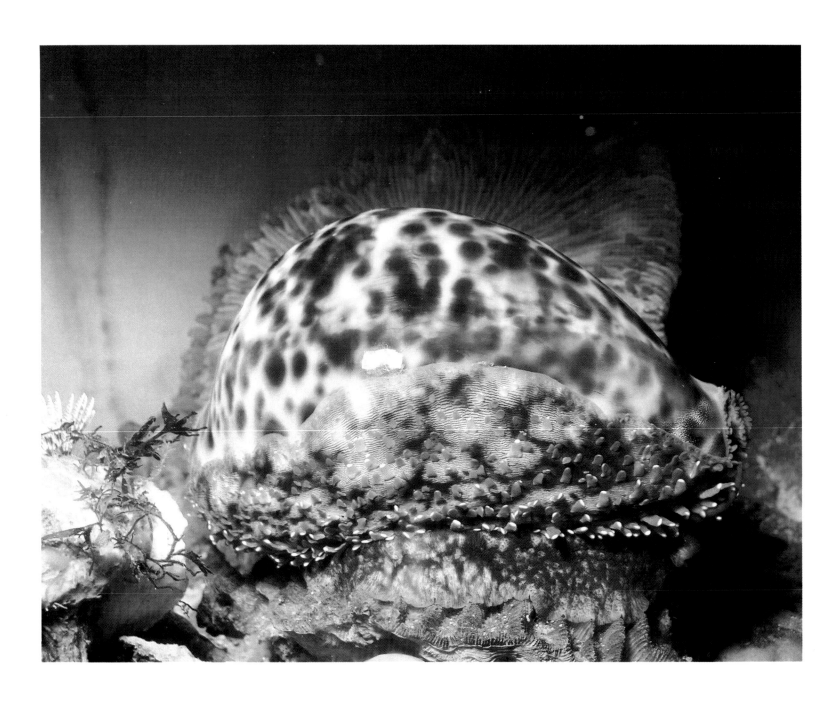

The millions of minute algae which live in the mantle tissues of this clam give rise to its brilliant colouring.

Australian fur seals were the basis of a lucrative fur industry when thousands were killed each year on the Bass Strait islands. They are now a protected species. (Following page.)

The Australian sea lion on Dangerous Reef, South Australia.

A great white shark patrols Dangerous Reef, South Australia. The most dangerous of sharks, this aggressive creature can grow to 11 metres in length.

Playful porpoises riding the waves.

The 9 metre killer whale (Orcinus orca), *most ferocious of all whales, is easily identified by its black and white body and large, triangular dorsal fin.*

The grey species of sea-snake (Aipysurus laevis). *Sea-snakes are often seen swimming on the surface waters in the more northern parts of the Barrier Reef.*

Marine turtles are a common sight in the Barrier Reef waters. (Following page.)

A juvenile moray eel sheltering on the Great Barrier Reef. Largely nocturnal, the moray seldom moves during the day except to poke its head out of its hiding place and snap at passing prey.

Green turtle (Chelonia mydas) *hatchlings at Heron Island. The Great Barrier Reef green turtle population may be the last of the world's great green turtle herds, most of the others being grossly over-exploited for their meat, oil, skin and shell.*

The loggerhead turtle (Caretta caretta) *is a large-headed marine turtle which can be found in all the world's oceans.*

The fearsome Australian stingray, one of the largest in the world.

The sea wasp (Chironex fleckeri), *one of the most venomous marine animals found in Australian waters. Despite their small size (about 30 centimetres) they possess a poison that can kill a man in ten minutes.*

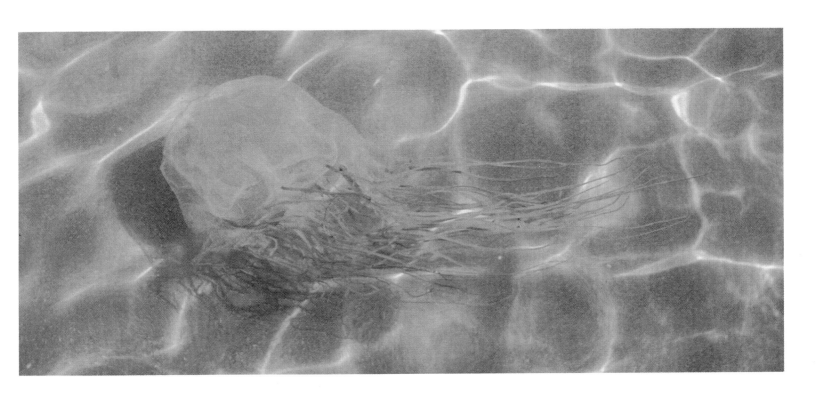

A native of warm waters, the blue-ringed octopus (Hapalochlaena maculosa) *has a lethal sting.*

The bluebottle has long tentacles which inflict an unpleasant sting. Fleets of them are often seen at beaches in Australia where they are frequently blown ashore by the prevailing winds.

Adelie penguins nest among ice slopes in the Australian Antarctic Territory.

The appealing fairy penguin, the smallest of all penguins and the only member of the penguin family to breed on the Australian continent.

The Adelie penguin (Pygoscelis adeliae). *(Previous page.)*

CITIES AND THE PEOPLE

The arrival of the First Fleet in 1788 brought together two of the most diverse peoples of the world: the eighteenth-century Englishmen and the Australian Aborigines.

In many ways Aboriginal society was the very antithesis of the world of the European. Governor Phillip observed no fences, agriculture or churches nor discerned any social stratification within the Aboriginal society. There was no concept of private ownership. All social, religious and economic activities were directed by an elaborate kinship system which not only placed people within the society but also all land, plants, animals and natural phenomena.

Whereas treaties were negotiated with the indigenous peoples of other British colonies, New South Wales was declared *terra nullius* or no-man's land. The Aboriginal people didn't appear to have any form of land ownership in the early settlers' eyes. This denial lead to the Aboriginal people being largely driven from their land. The consequences of these actions by the new settlers are only now being redressed.

In midsummer 1787 eleven ships sailed down the English Channel heading for a place that an eminent historian has called 'the biggest penitentiary on earth'. That fleet was carrying some 750 convicts to New South Wales and before that stream was to stop in the mid-nineteenth century about 160 000 felons were transported to the Great South Land. It was said of them that 'they left their Country for the Country's good'.

There has been some argument about the reasons for the settlement of the colony but it seems to be agreed that the loss of the North American colonies as a repository for convicts was the main one. It is also said that the lords of the Admiralty saw some advantage in a strategically placed settlement on the eastern shores of New Holland.

The early days

In January 1788 the First Fleet was in Botany Bay and there was disappointment with its inhospitable shores. By happy chance there was a bay only a short distance to the north, a harbour that Cook had named Port Jackson but had not entered. Governor Phillip described it as 'the finest harbour in the world' and modern-day Sydneysiders would argue strongly in support of that claim. It may not hold the '1000 ships of war' that Phillip thought it would safely hold but there is no greater sight than a thousand or more pleasure craft plying the sparkling waters of the harbour with the backdrop of the massive bridge and the world-renowned Opera House.

It is not to be thought that the miserable convicts and their unhappy guards were much taken with life in that remote spot. It was some two and a half years before another ship arrived from England and in that time convicts and guards alike were reduced to near-starvation. There was little familiar food that Europeans could find, except fish, and European plants did not flourish.

Fortunately, within a year or so of settlement Phillip found some more fertile land and at the end of 1789 Australia's first farmer, James Ruse, a freed convict, was tending his small plot of land near Parramatta. By the end of 1791 farming was flourishing so well in that area that Ruse was rewarded with 30 acres of land in the first land grant.

A couple of years later, John Macarthur, the stormy petrel of early politics in New South Wales, took up part-time farming at Parramatta on a land grant of about 100 acres and ten assigned convict workers. The house he commenced to build there in 1793 still stands and it is the oldest in Australia. Macarthur is regarded as the father of the Australian merino sheep industry. Perhaps his very able wife should be given at least equal credit because Macarthur himself was forcibly exiled in England for many years.

In the 1850s Bathurst was the centre of a great gold rush and Edward Hargraves was rewarded with £10 000 for his find. Within nine years of that discovery the population of New South Wales doubled. The 'roaring days' as they were called saw the now ghost town of Sofala with thirty grog houses to slake the thirst of 10 000 miners.

But even this paled into insignificance compared with the gold rushes in Victoria in the same decade when Victoria's population exceeded that of New South Wales. Bathurst became the headquarters of the famous coaching service of Cobb & Co., which was said to run about 30 000 horses in its heyday.

The first penal out-station in New South Wales was established at Newcastle in 1804 a few years after coal had been found near by. However, coal was not so important then as the great stands of cedar in the Hunter Valley or the immense oyster beds which when burnt yielded lime for the building trade in Sydney. Newcastle is now an iron and steel city of great importance to the Australian economy and one of the country's largest cities.

In 1883 a German-born boundary rider and two companions pegged out a claim in the Barrier Ranges in western New South Wales and thus was born the great silver, lead and zinc mines of Broken Hill. In 1885 what was to become the most powerful Australian company, the Broken Hill Proprietary Company Ltd, was established to work the immense metal lode. That deposit has produced great wealth for Australia but it seems to be giving out and the prosperity of the city is under threat.

A legacy of Broken Hill that will never be lost is that of strong and at times militant unionism. In the great strike of 1909 the unionists of the day were led by the famous Thomas Mann, a prominent English radical who was charged with sedition following a violent encounter with the police. He was acquitted and returned to England soon after but remains a folk hero in Broken Hill.

The great pioneering woman Caroline Chisholm, whose image appears on the $5 note, came to Sydney with her army husband in 1838. A year or two later, distressed by the condition of young girls in Sydney she commenced a home for ninety immigrant girls. She then went into the business of placing whole families into positions in the rural areas of New South Wales. Finally she established what was probably the first informal matrimonial agency in the State when hundreds of men wrote to her inquiring whether she would help in the finding of a wife.

Many ex-convicts were among the most prosperous businessmen of the infant colony of New South Wales but there were some who made their mark in the professions and the arts. William Redfern was a young naval surgeon sentenced to death in England in 1797. However, he was reprieved and transported. He became the outstanding doctor of the colony in the next twenty years, treating the rich and poor alike with skill and dedication. He was called the father of public medicine in the colony for his interest in the health of convicts.

Francis Greenway, another convict, was the architect of many fine Georgian buildings in Sydney. Macquarie was his mentor and his best known buildings are St James' Church and Hyde Park Barracks which stand close together in the heart of the city. Amazingly, the greatest architect in colonial Australia lies in an unmarked grave.

Sydney has now grown to Australia's largest city with about 3.5 million inhabitants. With a harbour to rival that of Rio de Janeiro and a larger population than Athens or Rome, Sydney is the continent's most international centre. Boasting theatres, restaurants, beaches and nightlife, the city lays claim to being the young and dynamic capital of Australia.

Expanding the colony

It was the presence of French ships under Admiral Baudin in 1802 that spurred Governor King into making a hurried annexation of Tasmania less than twenty years after the first settlement at Sydney. He planted small settlements at Risdon in 1803 and Port Dalrymple in 1804.

Apart from the strategic importance of Tasmania, King had in mind the development of the whaling, sealing and timber industries. He was also anxious to establish new convict settlements to take some of the more hardened criminals from New South Wales and from Norfolk Island when that outpost was temporarily abandoned.

Happily Tasmania retains the name of the Dutch navigator who discovered it in 1642. He himself named it Van Diemen's Land after the governor of Batavia who had sent him on his voyage. He landed at Blackman Bay on the eastern coast but then went on to New Zealand before sailing north to New Guinea to return to Batavia. He therefore has the dubious honour of being the first man to circumnavigate Australia without seeing any part of the mainland! He did, however, plant the Dutch flag even though the Dutch made no subsequent claim to it.

Life for the convicts of Tasmania was made deliberately hard because they were regarded as the most intractable of all and only the worst days on Norfolk could compare with the brutality of the regime. The toughest of all the prisons was at Macquarie Harbour on the west coast so it was not surprising that many tried to escape. Others more desperate simply committed murder, which at least meant a trip to Sydney for trial before hanging. Those who escaped into the wilderness of south-western Tasmania lived like animals and the toughest survived by slaughtering and eating the weakest or least vigilant.

Almost as infamous as Macquarie Harbour was the prison of Port Arthur. It was on land which was almost an island and across the narrow isthmus of Eaglehawk Neck a line of hounds was tethered on short chains so that no-one could pass between them. The rumour was spread that the nearby waters were infested by sharks so that Port Arthur had few escapees except for one remarkable Irishman, Martin Cash, who escaped four times in the 1840s and lived to farm quietly near Glenorchy.

After the hard early years things improved and a flow of free-settlers to the island State began but this had tragic consequences for the Aboriginal inhabitants of the island. There was nowhere for them to retreat and the estimated population of 5000 Aborigines in 1803 fell to about 500 twenty years later. In 1830 there occurred the infamous attempt to round up all the Aborigines to place them in a reserve. About 3000 armed whites conducted a drive across the whole colony for many weeks, resulting in two Aborigines being killed and two captured!

Hobart is a city the size of a big town. With less than 200 000 inhabitants and a wonderful setting between 'river and mountain' Hobart presents a rare successful blend of old and modern (Wrest Point was Australia's first legal casino). The beautifully preserved Georgian, Victorian and Edwardian buildings of the Battery Point area are one of the best preserved nineteenth-century townscapes in the country.

There has always been competition between the north and the south of Tasmania and the main city in the north, Launceston, can claim a history to rival that of Hobart. It is set in rich agricultural country and it produced hardy and adventurous men some of whom opened up the country across Bass Strait which became the State of Victoria. It was in Launceston that the Australian League for the Abolition of Transportation was established in 1849 and it quickly took root in the other colonies. Some claim this to be the first manifestation of an Australian national consciousness.

The early Australian colonies attracted some interesting and even famous figures but none more so than Sir John Franklin, who arrived in Hobart as governor in 1837. Man of action that he was, he was no match for the local hardheads who though him soft on convicts and dominated by his lively wife who acted more of the governor that he did. One of her most scatterbrained ideas was to rid Tasmania of snakes so she offered convicts a shilling a head for them! Her more lasting monuments are the Derwent Regatta and the first colonial Royal Society for scientific studies.

Tasmania's modern claim to fame is the central place it holds in the great environmental debate which has engaged Australia in the last decade. The State is well endowed with areas of rugged beauty and plant and animal life of tremendous scientific interest and, also, with men and women determined to see that the pristine beauty of their State is preserved. The heated debate with the developers goes on and all Tasmania's history suggests that it will be a battle royal.

However, the mellow beauty of the island which reminds many English people irresistibly of the Old Country has attracted many immigrants over the years and the preservation of the rich colonial inheritance makes it attractive to tourists.

Opening up the Top End

White settlement of the Northern Territory began in 1824 when a military outpost, Port Dundas, was established on Melville Island. Defence and trade were factors leading to its establishment but it proved to be unreliable for both.

Another attempt was made at Port Wellington on Raffles Bay three years later and this time showed greater promise when Macassan traders from Indonesia commenced to visit it. However, a decision made in London brought that settlement to an end in 1829.

In 1838 it was decided to try yet again and Captain Bremer planted the flag this time on an inner bay of Port Essington, which was named Victoria. The result was the same and in 1849 when cyclones and illness had taken their toll the survivors of the settlement of Victoria sailed away leaving as a legacy their dead and the remnants of their imported buffalo herds which were subsequently to run wild across the Top End.

In 1863 the Northern Territory came under South Australian control and that State made another attempt at white settlement at Palmerston in 1869 under the Surveyor-General Goyder known as 'Little Energy'. He was perceptive enough to acknowledge that 'we were to them [the Aborigines] in what appeared unauthorised and unwarranted occupation of the country ... territorial rights are strictly observed by natives'. Small-holder farming at subsistence level was the order of the day until Australia was crossed by the overland telegraph from Adelaide to London via Darwin and Java.

The dream of a tropical paradise was fading but the building of the telegraph line resulted in the discovery of gold at Pine Creek 200 kilometres south of Darwin. The rush lasted for only two years in the early 1870s but in that time a railway had been built to the coast at Port Darwin.

The building of the railway was largely done by thousands of Chinese coolies and that hardy and industrious race established a presence in the Territory which is important to this day. At the end of 1878 there were four times as many Chinese as Europeans. In 1966 Darwin elected the nation's first Chinese mayor.

In the early years of this century the first Greeks came to Darwin and in later years the islands of Kalymnos and Cyprus provided a new influx. Later still, Darwin took its share of the 'boat people' of Vietnam and with a new understanding of the culture of the indigenous Aborigines Darwin has become a melting pot in which different races are learning to live in harmony.

On Christmas Eve 1974 Tropical Cyclone Tracy demolished Darwin. Forty-nine people were killed in the city and over 90 per cent of the housing was destroyed or badly damaged. This brought an end to the old pioneering town with its colourful characters and tall stories.

Modern Darwin is a fast-growing city rapidly approaching 100 000 inhabitants. The locals still have a reputation for being tough but they are now more likely to be 'going bush' in air-conditioned comfort in a modern four-wheel-drive vehicle. It is a truly multiracial tropical city which has a reputation for getting on with the job. One cannot help feeling that it is a city that is still looking for its El Dorado.

The modern thriving city of Brisbane was settled in 1825 to receive convicts who had committed vicious crimes in Sydney. It was a harsh and squalid regime among the mangrove swamps of Moreton Bay and no free man was permitted to enter the area. One of the few landmarks remaining of those early days is the old windmill on Wickham Terrace which was originally fitted with a treadmill on which the convicts ground corn.

In the 1840s squatters began moving into the fertile Darling Downs and in 1859 Queensland became a separate colony. The convict era had ended in 1839 but development was slow. The great plains of Queensland were more suitable for cattle than sheep and the great distances involved prevented trade being developed until frozen exports commenced.

Development in Queensland has tended to spread out to the west from the coast with cities like Rockhampton and Townsville serving their own dependent hinterlands. It is not surprising in the circumstances that there is a strong separatist spirit in the north and west which regards Brisbane as being as remote as Sydney or Melbourne.

Rockhampton was a quiet rural centre in 1882 when the largest deposit of gold in Queensland was found at nearby Mount Morgan. When the gold was almost worked out, the town had a new lease of life with the discovery of the second largest deposit of copper in the State. However, in recent years the huge Bowen Valley coal deposits have come into production and Rockhampton has boomed.

In a similar way Townsville was a booming port at the end of the last century when the great goldfields of Charters Towers were in production. In recent years it has relied on being a service city for much of western Queensland and it also has large military establishments. Townsville is Australia's largest tropical city. It was one of the few Australian cities which suffered minor attacks by Japanese aircraft in World War II.

If there is one feature which distinguishes Queensland from the rest of Australia it is the style of its homes. With the abundance of suitable trees and the warm humid climate most of the early homes were of timber with surrounding wide verandahs standing on stilts to allow air circulation beneath. There are many fine mansions of this kind lovingly preserved but nowhere are they seen to better advantage than in Maryborough.

Mount Isa, one of the great mining cities of the world, is situated in north-western Queensland. This 'metropolis in the spinifex' has the largest underground mine in Australia, which puts it in world ranks in the production of silver, lead, zinc and copper. Reserves of metal already found in the area should last well into the next century.

Queensland at the end of the last century was the scene of great industrial confrontations that gave rise to the growth of the powerful Australian trade unions of today. In the great shearers strike of 1891 over 10 000 shearers massed in camps of a thousand or more men, many of them armed, and large numbers of police and troops moved into the pastoral areas. Fortunately, violence was limited but many arrests were made and many convictions followed.

Brisbane has over a million inhabitants and is the nation's third largest city after Sydney and Melbourne. Recently Brisbane was the host city to the Commonwealth Games and in 1988 will house Expo 88 in a sophisticated complex of modern buildings on the banks of the Brisbane River. Luxuriant tropical plants and elevated houses are the main characteristics of the city which spreads over rolling hill country. Brisbane is probably best known for its location near Australia's most famous holiday resort. The Gold Coast, including Surfers Paradise, is a major city and holiday destination in its own right. The vast stretches of golden sun-soaked ocean beaches were the original main attraction. The character has changed and it is increasingly seen as a retirement centre, especially for retirees from the colder southern States. Queensland's first legal casino is located on the Gold Coast and major fun parks and theme parks are thriving.

Moving to the west

A Scot, Captain Stirling, was the inspiration for the establishment of the beautiful city of Perth on the Swan River. He was sent from Sydney in 1827 to look for a suitable site for a new settlement in what is now the Northern Territory but on the way he sailed into the Swan River and fell in love with the country at first sight.

From that day Stirling devoted all his efforts to persuade the government to settle the Swan River district, which he suggested would be called 'Hesperia' or land looking to the setting sun.

The Swan River was settled in 1829 and colonists were given land in proportion to the amount of capital and labour they imported into the colony. It was a clear decision that no convicts were to be sent out and the colonists were mainly people from the ranks of the lesser gentry of England who had fought in the Napoleonic wars and hoped to improve their futures in a new land.

Unfortunately, too many of these men and their wives were not prepared to do the hard work required for success in a new land and the servants they brought out soon realised that they could do better by fending for themselves. The Aborigines whom it had been hoped would be quickly domesticated showed no enthusiasm for doing the menial work of the white masters. In 1851 the gentry gave in and called for convicts from the Mother Country and in the next twenty years over 10 000 of these unfortunates arrived.

The great wealth produced by the State of Western Australia did not come from the agricultural or pastoral pursuits followed by the earlier settlers. In 1893 it was the traditional luck of the Irish that saw the opening up of the so-called Golden Mile near Kalgoorlie. Paddy Hannan and his two Irish mates made their discovery at a time when the whole Australian economy was stagnating and men flocked from every State to the new El Dorado in the west. In ten years the population of Western Australia increased four-fold. By a great engineering feat water was directed to the fields by pipeline from near Perth—a distance of some 600 kilometres. The Kalgoorlie area has turned out to be one of the richest goldfields in the world and with world gold prices still booming the 'golden west' is making a great contribution to the nation's prosperity.

However, at a time when it seemed that gold had been worked out other minerals were found, including nickel in the Coolgardie area and iron ore in the tropical north of the State. This iron ore which goes to feed the great steel mills of Japan has led to the remarkable development of rail and port facilities in some of the harshest country in the world and many hardy and adventurous Australians work in the blistering heat to serve this massive mineral development. They are indeed in the same pioneer tradition as those who opened up Australia two hundred years ago.

After Canberra, Perth is the Australian city which owes much of its modern efficiency and look to careful town planning. With a population about the same as Adelaide, about one million, it enjoys dry Mediterranean weather. Perth's hot summer nights are tempered by the effects of a sea-breeze, the cooling 'Fremantle Doctor'. Perth shares with Sydney a magnificent natural setting for all the city, in this case the Swan River. Perth's seaport and a prosperous city in its own right, Fremantle played host to Australia's unsuccessful defence of the America's Cup in 1987.

'No convicts wanted'

The admirers of the city of Adelaide are loud in their praises of their prosperous capital on the shores of St Vincent Gulf, calling it the Athens of the South. Its detractors claim to see in it the home of the last wowsers and call it the city of churches and pubs.

The State had an interesting early history because it was the first settlement of white men in Australia planned and controlled almost entirely by merchant adventurers. Other settlements in Australia had sprung up on the initiative of the British government but the coast of South Australia was not strategically placed on the major sea routes of the time and the British government was satisfied to leave the development of the State in private hands.

From the beginning it was planned that only free men would breathe the air of the new State and despite all the difficulties of the early years no convicts were ever transported from England. The irony of this situation is that the man who developed the idea of a nation of free men in South Australia was Edward Wakefield, who wrote of his plans while a prisoner in Newgate prison in London serving a sentence for the abduction of a schoolgirl heiress.

It was fortunate that the British government intruded into the planning of the new colony to the extent of insisting that Colonel William Light would have the sole authority to decide upon the location of the new settlement. Against the wishes of Governor Hindmarsh, Light surveyed the site of the present city of Adelaide in 1836.

The new young State had many early difficulties because the heady air of freedom did not produce a great deal of human understanding and more time and money was spent in land speculation than development. In 1842 South Australia became an ordinary Crown Colony and the visionary dreams of Wakefield were at an end.

Only two or three years after settlement, there began arriving in Adelaide hundreds of hard-working Germans driven out of Prussia by religious persecution. They settled in their own colonies at Klemzig and Hahndorf and in later years they developed the rich vineyards at the Barossa Valley. These early industrious settlers contributed much to the economy of the infant settlement and especially in establishing the very important South Australian wine industry.

Before gold was discovered in the eastern States of Australia, South Australia gave the lead in the mining industry when copper was found at Kapunda in 1842 and at Burra in 1845. This led to a new wave of immigrants of Cornish origin and further waves of Cornish migrants came to South Australia to work when copper was later discovered at Moonta and Wallaroo. The gold rushes in the eastern States in the 1850s denuded South Australia of manpower for a time but later the State prospered by becoming a source of food for the goldfields.

Throughout its early history South Australia supported the efforts of the distinguished explorers like Sturt, Eyre and Stuart to open up new country in the north of the State but the results were always disappointing. No inland sea was discovered and the reports about the country were uniformly discouraging. However, Stuart did manage to cross Australia and reach the sea near Darwin in 1862.

The first export industry in South Australia developed even before the establishment of the settlement at Adelaide. Some of the early convict ships that sailed into Sydney

Harbour became whalers when they had discharged their human cargoes. American whalers from New England soon appeared and the name of Kangaroo Island's main river, American River, is a reminder of some of South Australia's earliest settlers.

Although South Australia has remained largely dependent upon primary production, this century has seen strong industrial development in the so-called Iron Triangle at the top of Spencer Gulf made up of the cities of Whyalla, Port Augusta and Port Pirie. This was made possible by a pipeline from the Murray River built in 1944.

In recent years, Adelaide has leapt into international prominence by staging the Formula One motor-racing Grand Prix and by the conversion of its Victorian railway station into a grand casino. Adelaide is now a city of a million people. It is the city of stone houses and leafy gardens and the city of cultural festivals.

Victoria is the smallest of the Australian States and comparatively the most fertile, which makes it surprising that it was not settled earlier. It remained a part of New South Wales until 1851, which perhaps accounts for the love-hate relationship which exists between the two. The rivalry has always been intense and manifests itself to this day in the struggle between Sydney and Melbourne to become the acknowledged financial capital of the Commonwealth.

The first white settlement of Victoria occurred in 1803 at the time of the fears aroused by the presence of the French ships in southern Australian waters. Three hundred convicts and their guards under David Collins were landed at Sorrento near the mouth of Port Phillip Bay. While that area may now be regarded as a pleasant holiday resort it was no place for a settlement. Collins quickly obtained the permission of Governor King to withdraw and he was ordered to join the infant settlement at Hobart. A second unsuccessful attempt to set up a convict establishment on Western Port Bay lasted only two years.

The real drive to settle in Victoria came from the merchant adventurers and pastoralists in the north of the infant colony of Tasmania. The first of these was Edward Henty who went to Portland in 1834; a year later John Batman went to the head of Port Phillip Bay and found a place he thought suitable as a 'village'. This was to become the great city of Melbourne but Batman, in the true entrepreneurial spirit of the times, negotiated his farcical 'treaty' with local Aborigines by which he purported to succeed to 240 000 hectares of land in exchange for some blankets, axes and other trinkets.

Hot on the heels of Batman came Fawkner, the son of a convict transported for fourteen years in 1801. Fawkner himself was a convict but such was the egalitarian spirit of early Australia that the name became one of the most respected in the land.

It was not long before the central government in Sydney had to exert its authority over the warring white chieftains at Melbourne and 'Superintendent' La Trobe arrived in 1839 to extend the 'King's Peace'. He remained to become governor of the new State and presided over its growth until 1854.

Victoria comes of age

The day after the new colony was proclaimed in 1851 gold was discovered at Warrandyte in the nearby hills. In the following decade Melbourne was said to be the fastest growing city in the world. In 1873 the English novelist Anthony Trollope pronounced it to be 'the undoubted capital of all Australia' and most Australians suspect that is how most Melburnians still see it. In one respect at least, the claim must be said to be undisputed because Melbourne was the home of the brand of football called Australian Rules.

Most Australians would also be prepared to concede that the most famous meeting spot in the country is 'under the clocks' at Flinders Street Station, which is across the road from that other famous landmark, Young and Jackson's Hotel. The building is humble by any standards but it stands boldly near the Cathedral and houses 'Chloe', the most famous nude painting in Australia.

Another famous landmark in the central city district is the Exhibition Building which housed the International Exhibition of 1880. In 1901 it was the scene of the first sitting of Parliament of the Commonwealth of Australia.

Though no city in Victoria was ever to equal Melbourne, Ballarat and Bendigo became exciting places during the gold-rush days and these remain important provincial centres. Ballarat is proud to claim that when the internationally known courtesan Lola

Montez danced there she was showered with gold nuggets. When chided by the editor of the *Ballarat Times* she is said to have horsewhipped him in public.

These were nothing if not fiery times. The miners were men of independent spirit and anger was aroused by the fees charged for mining licences and the sometimes brutal methods adopted to collect them.

This led to what was undoubtedly the most significant rebellion against government in Australian history. In 1854, under an Irishman, Peter Lalor, a number of miners undertook rudimentary military training and a crude stockade was built at Eureka. When the armed showdown with the troopers occurred thirty defenders of the stockade and five attackers were killed. Lalor lost an arm in the fight. Thirteen men were subsequently charged with treason but such was the public sympathy for the miners' case that all were acquitted. Lalor entered politics and was later Speaker of the Victorian Legislative Assembly. The name of Eureka has become a powerful catalyst in the trade union and republican movements in Australia.

When the heady days of goldmining had passed, Victoria was blessed with the discovery of great brown coal deposits in the Latrobe Valley east of Melbourne. These deposits supply most of the State's electrical power and to add to this natural bounty quantities of natural gas and crude oil are being developed off the Gippsland coast.

Melbourne's reputation is as the financial capital of the nation. With over half of Australia's major companies based there, it is a tradition of 'boardroom and clubs'. Melbourne is claimed to be the fashion capital but this too is in a rather conservative style. The spring horseracing carnival, culminating in the nation's most lucrative race, the Melbourne Cup, is a mecca for the fashion conscious.

The national capital

The national capital which was once described as 'six villages in search of a city' is now hailed as a place of great beauty. The central integrating lake is named Burley Griffin after the American architect and town planner who won a worldwide planning contest a few years after New South Wales yielded the territory to the federal government 1909.

Canberra has a unique claim to fame connected with the way in which it was chosen as Australia's capital. In the years leading up to the establishment of the Commonwealth there was great rivalry between the two most populous States, New South Wales and Victoria. Neither State would give the honour of being capital of Australia to the other and the smaller States were against Sydney and Melbourne, so the American example was followed and the decision was that a sparsely settled area be found for the infant capital. In fact, such was the distrust between the two States that it was decided to make special provision in the new Constitution that the seat of government would be in New South Wales 'but not less than 100 miles from Sydney'.

As a sop to Melbourne it was decided that that city would be home to the Australian Parliament until the new capital was ready for occupation. That did not come about until 1927, by which time some cynics say that Melburnians were glad to say goodbye to the politicians.

So it was that in 1927 the politicians and public servants brought a new kind of society to the limestone plains. This undulating landscape had seen few changes in the hundred or so years since the squatters with their convict shepherds first pushed down from Sydney towards the Murrumbidgee and the high plains. A small convict gaol can still be seen at Lanyon Homestead near Canberra and the Governor-General's residence, Yarralumla, and Duntroon House at the Royal Military College were the country mansions of two pioneering wool barons.

Canberra has a further dubious claim to fame: that it has no elected municipal or territorial government and sixty years after Parliament first came to Canberra self-government seems as far away as ever.

Canberra is the largest inland city and with a population of over a quarter of a million is exceeded in size only by the five State capitals and Newcastle. The city is growing as a tourist centre as the number and variety of national public buildings increase. The crown of these buildings will be the new National Parliament House, due to be opened by Queen Elizabeth in 1988.

Sadar—the last of the Afghan camel drivers at Alice Springs. Early settlements in this area were serviced by regular camel train from Port Augusta. When the railway was completed in 1929, the service became known as 'The Ghan', after the Afghan camel drivers it had replaced.

Buffalo hunting in the Northern Territory. These destructive animals were first introduced into the region from Timor in 1825 Because of their wallowing habits they cause severe environmental damage to swamps and lagoons. (Previous page.

See the country in style—a camel tour at Alice Springs. (Page 257.)

Alice Springs, a modern well-maintained town right in the heart of the MacDonnell Ranges in the Red Centre of Australia.

Las Vegas by the sea—Diamond Beach Casino, a strikingly modern casino and hotel complex in Darwin.

A new Darwin has grown out of the ruins of Cyclone Tracy which struck in 1974. Now a modern city, Darwin's prosperity is based largely on the mineral wealth of the Northern Territory. It also benefits from tourism.

Boats and other floating craft are constructed out of beer cans at the Beer Can Regatta held in Darwin each June.

The Kuranda tourist train takes visitors on a spectacular ride through the Atherton Tableland, Queensland.

Smoko for a Northern Territory buffalo hunter.

The sugarcane train takes visitors through more than 40 hectares of pineapples, mangoes, avocados, nuts, spices and sugarcane at the Sunshine Plantation near Nambour in Queensland. ►

The Story Bridge spans the Brisbane River which wanders lazily through the city and suburbs out into Moreton Bay. ◄

Artesian bores provide water in areas in western Queensland where sheep, cattle and sometimes people could not survive on natural surface water supplies alone.

The superb climate and fine harbour get many Sydneysiders afloat every weekend. Yacht racing is of a high standard and consistently produces winning international boats and crews.

City Hall, Brisbane's best known building, is dwarfed by the modern skyscrapers that dominate the skyline.▼

Sunset over Sydney—seen across the finest natural harbour in the world.

Fireworks burst over the Sydney Opera House, a controversial architectural masterpiece which cost $102 million to build.

Sydney Harbour Bridge, known affectionately as the Old Coathanger, was opened in 1932 and is the only direct link to the developing twin city of North Sydney and the northern suburbs.

Berowra Waters on the Hawkesbury River—near Sydney—a boating paradise. Majestic, unspoiled scenery gives the Hawkesbury its reputation for being the most beautiful river on the Australian continent. ▼

The Scenic Skyway offers a spectacular view of the famous Three Sisters rock formation in the Blue Mountains, New South Wales. ◄

Visitors enjoying 'boats for hire' in the Royal National Park, south of Sydney. The second national park to be proclaimed anywhere in the world, this park covers 15 000 hectares. ▼

The High Court of Australia, officially opened in 1980 (left), blends harmoniously with the National Library on the shores of Lake Burley Griffin, Canberra.

A rainbow slants through the spectacular Captain Cook Memorial Jet on Lake Burley Griffin, Canberra. The Jet, which was built by the Commonwealth government to commemorate Cook's discovery of Australia in 1770, shoots a column of water 137 metres into the air. ◄

The Australian War Memorial is the venue for the Anzac Day services in Canberra and many Australians share in these solemn moments of remembrance.

Canberra, Australia's national capital, viewed from the summit of Mount Pleasant. Only seventy-five years ago this was open farming and grazing country; now it is one of the world's best known fully planned cities.

The Victorian Arts Centre, focus for the visual and performing arts in Melbourne.

274

Melbourne by night. Founded by John Batman in 1835, Melbourne today has an unruffled elegance and style all its own. ▲

Moomba, Melbourne's boisterous March festival, is a fun time for all.

South Melbourne Beach. Going to the beach is almost a religious ritual for the majority of Australians, especially city dwellers.

Houseboats on Lake Eildon, Victoria's largest man-made lake. Surrounded by the beautiful foothills of the Alps, the lake is well stocked with trout, Murray cod and redfin.

The Yarra River flows unhurriedly past the bustling, compact city centre of Melbourne. The city's architecture is a fine mixture of elegant concrete and glass edifices and magnificent colonial buildings such as the Flinders Street railway station on the right. ◄

Hobart, the capital of Tasmania, is a picturesque blend of riverscape and mountain vistas, a mixture of old and new settlement.

The impressive GPO in Hobart, Tasmania. Hobart has a wealth of beautiful early colonial buildings, more than ninety of them having National Trust classification.

Port Arthur, Tasmania, is the only substantial convict ruin in Australia and has been preserved as a scenic reserve. ◄

Richmond Bridge, straddling the calm waters of the Coal River in Tasmania, is Australia's oldest bridge. It was built by convicts between 1823 and 1825 and is said to be haunted by their cruel overseer whom they killed. ▶

The spires of St Peter's Cathedral seen from the pretty Pennington Gardens in Adelaide. ▼

The superb Adelaide Festival Centre, the city's major venue for the performing arts, overlooks the Torrens River. ▲

Chateau Yaldara winery at Lyndoch, South Australia, in the picturesque Barossa Valley, Australia's premier wine-producing region. ▼

The Adelaide Hills—a blend of gently rolling mountains, market gardens and orchards, with farm buildings nestled in the valleys. ►

A day's outing at the Fitzroy Crossing racetrack in the Kimberleys, Western Australia. (Following page.)

Easygoing Perth—capital of Western Australia. The clear blue Swan River winds its way through the city centre which is ringed by beautiful gardens, parks and reserves.

Boating on the Swan River is a popular pastime in Perth.

Acknowledgements

The publishers wish to acknowledge the valuable assistance of the Australian Picture Library staff and the people whose material is held by the Australian Picture Library.

Australian Picture Library/VOLVOX: pages 245 and 246-7

Australian Picture Library/ZEFA: pages 63, 228 and 229.

Henry Ausloos: pages 44 above and 238 below.

Douglass Baglin: pages 64-5 below, 66, 68, 107 below, 121 above, 146 above, 163, 165, 177, 178 below, 183, 260 above and 262.

John Baker: pages 41, 112 above, 116 above right, 120, 145 below, 152, 158 below, 164, 181, 184, 185 above, 186, 193, 194, 198 above, 199 above, 233, 273, 274 and 283.

Robert Berthold: pages 101 above, 145 above and 224 above left and below.

Roy Bisson: page 119 below.

William Caram: page 195.

John Carnemolla: pages 20 below, 22, 24 above right, 25, 26-7, 28, 29, 32 above, 33, 37, 38, 40 above, 42, 44 below, 64-5 above, 68 above, 70, 73, 74, 84-5, 106, 107 above right, 108, 113, 116 below, 122-3, 124-5, 126 above left, 137, 139 below, 153, 158 above, 159, 162 below, 168, 178 above, 185 below, 189 below, 202, 206 below, 218-19, 231 above, 234-5, 240-1, 243 below, 244 above, 258-9, 261 below, 264, 267, 269 below, 270, 271, 272, 285 and 286-7.

Dive 2000: page 243 above.

Ron Dorman: pages 104-5, 110-11, 143 below, 190-1 and 204-5.

Colin Driscoll: pages 20 above, 24 above left, 238 above and 244 below.

Richard Eastwood: pages 280 and 281.

Wally Glover: page 189 above right.

Ronald Gordon: page 266.

Ken Griffiths: pages 109 and 112 below.

Dallas and John Heaton: pages 17, 21, 30-1, 58 below, 59, 60, 61 and 265 above.

Leigh Hemmings: pages 35 above and 166-7.

Wally Herzfeld: pages 121 below, 200 below and 201.

Raymond Hoser: page 78 below.

Owen Hughes: pages 118, 149, 154-5, 162 above, 208, 260 below and 288 above.

Wade Hughes: page 36 above.

Roderick Hulsbergen: pages 268-9.

Steve Hynes: pages 101 below, 102, 116 above left and 279.

Alan Jones: pages 62, 98-9 and 282 below.

Tony Joyce: page 199 below.

Noeline Kelly: pages 117 above, 123, 126 above right and below, 127, 143 above left, 157, 182, 188, 192, 196, 200 above, 203, 206 above, 217 and 275.

Gary Lewis: pages 34 below, 40 below, 43, 58 above, 65 above, 67, 68 below, 76, 77, 87 below, 179, 197, 207, 248, 261 above, 263, 276 below and 284.

S. W. Lowry: pages 107 above left, 114-15, 148 below and 277 below.

Jim McKay: pages 24 below, 236 and 237.

Middenway & Jones: page 180 below.

Greg Miller: page 141 right.

Robert Nelson: page 146 below.

Outback Photography: page 139 above.

Profile Photography: pages 156 and 288 below.

Fritz Prenzel: pages 18, 19, 23, 32 below, 45, 46, 65 below, 79, 117 below, 138 above left, 138 below, 140, 141 left, 142, 143 above right, 144, 160-1, 180 above, 187, 198 below, 232, 265 below and 268 below.

Norman Quinn: pages 227 below and 231 below.

Derek Roff: pages 34 above, 35 below, 39, 47, 48, 49, 69, 71, 72, 74, 78 above, 80-1, 82, 83, 87 above, 96-7, 100 above, 147, 148 above and 150-1.

Joseph Spiteri: pages 138 above right and 189 above left.

Paul Steel: pages 103, 119 above, 276-7 and 282 above.

Laurie Thomas: page 278.

Steve Vidler: pages 100 below and 257.

Mike Warman: page 36 below.

Bill Wood: pages 220, 221, 222, 223, 224 above right, 225, 226, 227 above, 230, 239 and 242.

Index

Numerals in *italics* denote colour photographs.